A Song for

Lost Angels

A Song for
Lost Angels

HOW DADDY AND PAPA
FOUGHT TO SAVE THEIR FAMILY

Kevin Fisher-Paulson

FEARLESS BOOKS

First Edition
January 2014

Fearless Books
PO Box 4199, Napa CA 94558
www.fearlessbooks.com

The story told in these pages is true, but some
names have been changed to protect the
privacy of individuals.

Design & Typography:
D. Patrick Miller

ISBN: 978-0-9888024-2-1

Library of Congress Control Number:
2013951087

TABLE OF CONTENTS

PUBLISHER'S PREFACE

LIKE MANY denizens of the self-employed underworld, I hold "office hours" in a coffeehouse. Driving from my home in Napa, California a few miles away to my favorite haunt most mornings, I've gotten in the habit of listening to public radio station KQED's "Perspective" series. These short, audible essays are written by KQED listeners and are open to anyone in northern California with a good story or angle on life to relate.

On the morning of April 2, 2012, I was listening when a fellow named Kevin Fisher-Paulson began his Perspective with the words, "I'm a lucky man. I've already had the worst day of my life."

He went on to relate how, on that awful day, he and his husband Brian lost their triplets — whom they had nursed into health from the brink of death during a year of dedicated foster care — to a court system that returned the children to their schizophrenic, drug-addicted birth mother. That's the story of this book, which is told in the following pages with grace, dignity, and a surprisingly generous dose of humor.

I confess that what really got my attention that morning, though, was another line in Kevin's report. Commenting on how surviving the worst day of his life had emboldened him to take "wild chances," Kevin mentioned that he had recklessly "sent off books to publishers, knowing that one more rejection letter doesn't compare to losing children."

Hmm, I thought. I got in touch with Kevin the next day, finding out that he was a published writer, veteran gay rights activist, former handbag salesman, *and* a Captain in the San Francisco Sheriff's Department. (From a publisher's purely mercenary point of view, this story was already looking Too Good.) He told me that he had indeed sent around a proposal for this very book, to no avail. So I offered my professional services to review and reshape his proposal, which I've done hundreds of times for writers over my twenty-plus years as an editor and publishing consultant.

It was not my intention, at that time, to develop this book for my own imprint, under which I publish only a few titles yearly. My usual subject matter is contemporary spirituality; that wasn't entirely irrelevant to Kevin's story, but certainly wasn't its focus. More to the point, though, was my conviction that this book deserved major national exposure of the sort that mainstream, New York-based publishing houses still provide best. That meant sending out his improved proposal to literary agents, of whom I knew a handful well enough to keep Kevin's work off the bottom of their slushpiles. If that effort came to naught, I told him, we'd look at the fallback position of independent publishing, possibly even establishing his own imprint.

As it happened, even I was taken aback by the responses received from querying the agents I knew. Almost without exception, they regretfully declined even to examine the proposal, on the grounds that Kevin had too little "platform." (This is a buzzword in the book biz that can best be translated for civilians as "How famous are you already?") This defeatist attitude is not really the fault of agents. Most of them have simply tired of sending worthwhile properties to major houses only to hear that they're not taking on new projects, particularly nonfiction projects, by writers without platform.

If you're a Kardashian, a high-profile headline-grabber, or a movie star who couldn't write your way out of a 100% recycled paper sack, you've got platform — and that means you can easily get a writer assigned to you and get "your" book published. But just being a good writer with an important story to tell isn't usually enough these days.

Eventually I decided that Kevin's obvious talent and

remarkable history provided plenty of platform for me, and that's how *A Song for Lost Angels* ended up as a Fearless Books release. In fact, it's the "charter title" in our new Personal History Project, in which we will be scanning proposals, blogs, the airwaves, the psychic ether, and any other medium we happen across for compelling memoirs of unusual significance.

As I've told many writers endeavoring to tell their personal histories, my first rule for effective memoirs is *"It's not about you"* — meaning that a personal history must connect so well with readers that they feel it's about them. On that score, Kevin's book is about a great many potential readers: gay spouses, anyone who has dealt with the foster/adoption system, anyone who has confronted overt discrimination, parents of every description, and even those who live in thrall to their dogs.

Besides exploring meaningful issues that transcend a writer's personal history, a successful memoir must be powerfully written, and that is also true of *A Song for Lost Angels*. In a concise rendering that's neither self-important nor sensational, Kevin has penned a painfully true story that will actually make you laugh, cry, and occasionally sputter with outrage.

This book is being published in a time when gay marriage is finally breaking through the bonds of an historically stupid national prejudice in America. That means the rights and struggles of gay-parented families are due for greater exposure. It's a long shot to get a large audience for a book released by a micro-publisher, but I've done it before. One just has to be willing to take wild chances every now and then.

Publishing has never been a fair, equitable, or even demonstrably sane business. Given the contemporary obsessions with celebrities, sensationalism, and zombification, nowadays there are too many good, solid books by new writers falling through the cracks of an increasingly fractured industry.

But not this one.

D. Patrick Miller
Publisher, Fearless Books
October 2013

DEDICATION

This book is dedicated to my husband,
Brian Fisher-Paulson, who will always be
the best Papa in the world.

CHAPTER 1

Feast of Saint Serafina

"A man does not have to be an angel in order to be a saint."
−ALBERT SCHWEITZER

July 19, 1999

BRIAN SLID into the near end of the second red leather booth at Yet Wah's, the Chinese restaurant that we had been eating at for eight years. He always left me at the far end, so that I could see the door; that little part of me is always a cop. It was a smarmy kind of place, on the second floor of a strip mall. There were big booths done in burgundy naugahyde, and there's just something about a booth that makes even a strip mall restaurant feel intimate. Since Diamond Heights is the foggiest neighborhood in all of San Francisco, it was like eating in the clouds. Irene, our waitress, had brought us a carafe of cheap blush wine. I poured a glass for each of us, and Brian said, "To your birthday tomorrow?"

Tomorrow would be the Feast of Saint Uncumber, patron saint of bearded women, and my 41st Earth anniversary. "Not yet. I'm having my mid-life crisis."

Brian is thin with dark hair. Fine lines have descended on his cheekbones, which only make him more handsome than when I met him in 1985. He rolled his dark brown eyes. "You mean your *annual* mid-life crisis. For your fortieth, you went skydiving with Tim and then you got a tattoo. How are you going to top that?"

I shrugged, picked up my glass and clinked it against his. "To us. And whatever middle age brings us." The blush had lost nothing of its sweet yet sour flavor. I picked up the chopsticks, tapped out a drumbeat on the tablecloth.

"No Tim?" Irene asked. No, we had the night off. Tim was our oldest friend in the world. He had moved onto our couch when he was going cold turkey from heroin, and never quite got around to moving out. Tim was a manic-depressive recovering addict living with AIDS. Brian met him in Maine and I had known him since our New York days. He was the first of my friends to be diagnosed, and yet the one who had lived longest through the plague. Together he and I had been founding members of the first chapter of ACTUP (The AIDS Coalition to Unleash Power) back in New York. When Brian and I moved out to San Francisco, Tim came along, establishing himself as the third member of our couple. But having recently

2

formed a coven, he was not there for our weekly family dinner.

Irene did not hand us menus; that hadn't been necessary for quite a while. A few minutes later, she brought us pot stickers with spicy mustard to start, followed by Brian's order of General Kung Pao Chicken and Pork-Fried Rice, and my Garlic String Beans. I struggled to pinch a pot sticker with the white plastic chopsticks, and bit down, the mustard tickling my tongue. Irene had given the two of us lessons in chopsticks a few years ago. Brian picked it up in two seconds, as he does any new dance routine. I still struggled to pinch the food, but believed I was virtuous in defeat.

As always, I flicked away at his chicken and rice with the chopsticks, until I gave up and dove in with a fork. This explains why he is so thin, and why I must compensate for my thickness with charm. A half hour later, every plate empty, as well as the carafe, Irene brought the check over with two fortune cookies. I picked the one pointing at me. Brian awaited his fate.

On cue, he asked, "Well, what does it say?"

"Help! I'm a prisoner in a Chinese Bakery!"

He groaned, as he always does. "Now, what does it really say?"

"Your children respect your wisdom."

And that was the moment when everything changed.

Oh, yes, a lot of thinking had gone into it: about how I was in my forties, how I didn't know what my life meant, how I didn't want to get old without... what?

Maybe such questions are more difficult for a gay man, maybe not. I had led many lives: activist, poet, handbag salesman, sheriff's deputy, and all-around *bon vivant*. I had made many friends. Sadly, many of those friends who had constituted a kind of family were either dead or dying, and slowly rising in me was the realization that what meant most to me was family. I wanted another family, a "forever" one.

"Brian, I want to have children," I blurted. "I think I'm meant to."

Brian put his chopsticks down, picked up his glass, narrowed his eyes and looked off in the distance as if he had known for a long time that this challenge would come up, but had still not figured out how to answer. What I later comprehended was that for me, fatherhood would simply be a new option; for Brian it would mean a choice between continuing his life as a dancer or starting something else entirely. For me, it would still mean coming home every night. But Brian spent most of the year on tour to such exotic dance locations as Iowa and Wisconsin. And he did not see family as a traveling concept.

We are an unlikely couple. He is a creative, nurturing artist; I am a pragmatic and blunt cop. We'd been in love for fourteen years, having met over my cousin Rita's lasagna dinner in Jersey City. It was the only successful blind date I had with anybody. A month later we moved in together, into a coldwater flat above a funeral home that we shared with a bunch of starving dancers, actors, and singers, kind of like La Bohème with a Jersey accent.

In 1991, both of our careers came to a full stop. He quit dancing for a while and I managed to get fired from yet another retail chain. The year that our Christmas tree committed suicide, we moved out west to San Francisco for a fresh new start. He joined a modern dance company, ODC/San Francisco, and despite all of my unsuitability for the role, I joined the San Francisco Sheriff's Department. We moved into a one-bedroom condominium with three dogs, and eventually Tim joined us.

And here I was asking Brian to be the father of my children. He smiled his stage smile, and for a second I thought he would just say no. He hesitated a little, and then looked me straight in the eye. "As long as I'm with ODC, they expect me to tour. But you're right. I can't ask you to wait until I finally retire in five years or so."

"Which is close to a hundred in gay years," I retorted, crunching on the fragments of cookie. I picked up a crumb with my abandoned chopsticks.

"Okay, we start. Right away," he lifted his wine glass, clinked mine with it, and said, "To family."

THE NEXT morning, I called a senior deputy, a lesbian I knew who had just adopted. "Who did you use for an agency?" I asked, sipping my morning latté.

"The Black Adoption Network."

"Do we qualify? Not being black and all? Even though I'm shanty Irish, Brian is distantly related to the Mayflower."

"They don't care, so long as you give the kids a good home. You sure this is the route you want to go?"

"Yes," I said, "we're not going to do surrogacy, as neither of us feel that our contribution to the gene pool is all that important." We had already decided against foreign adoption when we learned that America was importing white, Latino and Asian children for adoption but was still exporting many black children to Germany, the Netherlands, Canada, and other countries simply because the average adopting American still focused on race.

"Then you're in the right place."

I called the agency and got a receptionist. We received the first of hundreds of pages of applications.

The process was long. We knew that our one-room condo in Diamond Heights was too small, so we searched and searched until we found a bungalow in the Crocker Amazon, the neighborhood San Francisco forgot. It is an arts and craft style home, built in 1916, with a real chimney and wooden floors. The real estate agent explained that the word *bungalow* is originally Hindi and means "low house with thatched roof." But to me bungalow meant *cozy*. And the minute we stepped into the living room with the gumwood and fireplace, with two little milk glass windows on either side, Brian said, "This is the kind of home in which you can raise a family." The cove ceilings were perfect; the stucco was perfect; the lilacs in the backyard were perfect. The only things we didn't like were the size of the mortgage and the fact that exterior of the house had been painted mustard and brown.

A week after purchasing it, we painted the bungalow Batman blue. Growing up in a gray and brick row house in South Ozone Park, I had promised myself that someday I would paint my own home the color of my favorite super-hero. The neighbors were aghast. Our fur babies, Miss Grrrl, Wolfcub, and Diva were all delighted by having their very own yard, full of lilacs, calla lilies and overgrown grass. The inside of the house with its huge kitchen and tiny office was equally unkempt, but it was the kind of house where you always felt at home.

In the meantime, we filled out all those foster/adoption forms. A social worker walked into our house, and examined everything from the contents of our medicine cabinet to the pedigree of our dogs. Turning up her nose, she asked, "Have they had their rabies shots? Have any of them ever attacked anyone?"

"They've had their shots, but it's hard to say about attacking someone," I answered. "They're Pekingese. Their idea of an attack is licking your hand 'til you give them cheese."

She frowned, and then asked about Tim as if he weren't right there in the room. "Wouldn't he be dangerous? Your form indicated he was manic depressive."

Tim smiled. "I've had my shots."

I added, "And he's in a Twelve Step program, and seeing a psychiatrist, and on medication. Otherwise he's as normal as you or me."

"It's just a little unusual. Three gay men living in a house, one of them not really stable." She fretted her brows, wrote something in her little black notebook, and left.

And then we waited.

TWO YEARS passed without the agency coming up with a single child for us. During that time, my mother, Nurse Vivian, passed away from ovarian cancer. I went to Florida for her final days. Even while dying, she remained Nurse Vivian: "Kevin, bury me in the mint chiffon dress. You know, the one I wore to Donald's wedding? It seemed like such a shame that I never got to wear it again." She told me to go back to the apartment, that she wanted me to get some sleep, and at five in the morning, the phone rang.

I answered, and a doctor said, "I am sorry to tell you that your mother passed away in her sleep."

Pop and I brought her home to Yaphank to be laid to rest. For a time my grief occupied me, but then I went back to California and the issue of the adoption to no avail. I called the agency once or twice a month, but they never had a prospective placement for us. I gave up several times, but Brian never did.

"All in good time," he said about ten times a week. Brian had crossed the Rubicon that night in Yet Wah's. Like his gymnastics, like his dancing on Broadway, whatever he pursued he believed in completely, and he had no doubt that we were on the road to parenthood.

Me, I got more and more OCD, which is to say that I imagined the worst possible outcomes. In the meantime, I organized the spices. I alphabetized the cheese. I collated the thirteen cartons of comic books into numerical order.

Tim stayed busy, fighting the disease, fellow coven members, the doctors, and his inner demons. His health went downhill. He couldn't eat because of intestinal complications, and he had shingles, and he began to feel that he was a burden on us. So one night, in the tiny bedroom with a draft, he attempted suicide with what he thought was a bottle of chlonodine and a bottle of lithium. Turned out he actually downed a bottle-full of Viagra (yes, yes, I know: that would have made one stiff corpse). We got him to San Francisco General Hospital, and a charcoal milkshake later, he survived. Afterward he knew that he needed to change direction so he went into rehab again. In a lockup ward in Los Angeles he met the love of his life. When he returned, he moved out to an apartment in the Mission District, leaving the blue bungalow to us, the three dogs, and whatever children might come into our future.

I'm Irish. That translates to superstitious. We started going back to church, because even if our own faith was shaky, we wanted our kids to have some starting point in discussions of theology and ethics. I suggested to Brian, "Let's go to a different church every Sunday until we find one that we feel comfortable in."

"Where shall we start?" he asked.

"With the Catholics, of course. Then we can try the Metropolitan Community Church and the Unitarians. If all else fails, we can always join Tim's coven." On the first Sunday of our experiment, the Feast of the Epiphany, we walked into Most Holy Redeemer Church, in the Castro District. It had a big banner over the entrance that read "God's INCLUSIVE Love," and pictures of the parish serving meals to the homeless, and working with persons with AIDS, and even marching in the Pride Parade.

We sat in the back, and the sunlight burned brightly through the stained glass. Before the mass started, the priest asked any newcomers to stand up, and we did, and about ten people shook our hands. Soon after the opening hymn, the choir launched into the Gloria. As we came to the chorus (where in my youth the altar boys rang the bells) the parishioners pulled their keys out of their pockets and started jangling them. It sounded like a crazy carillon. I leaned over to Brian. He nodded and I whispered, "We're home."

We got knee-deep in the parish, baking pies for the Wednesday night supper for the homeless and singing with the choir on Sundays. The great thing about Most Holy Redeemer was that no one put much emphasis on *faith*. It was all about *work*. And that work kept us busy as we waited on the adoption agency.

One Sunday at church, I lit a candle and asked, "Is this really going to happen? Is there a better way to approach this?"

We walked out of the church and over to the Castro Street Fair. While shopping for knick-knacks, I saw a sign that read "A BETTER WAY: FOSTER/ADOPTION AGENCY." The coincidence bell dinged in my head. If they advertised in the Castro, this agency had to like gay people. Brian and I signed our name to a list, and got a phone call the next day.

They sent us a very nice social worker, a heavyset red-headed woman with brilliant green eyes named Meredith

St. Jacques, who gave us even more paperwork to fill out, and who also examined our house, but a little more gently. Meredith ignored the dust bunnies, saying, "How cute your dogs are!" She even affirmed the unmowed lawn: "What fun that would be for the kids!" She smiled, wrote something in a little pink notebook, gathered up her overstuffed purse and left.

And then on March 31, 2003 we got the call from her: "Congratulations! You are officially eligible to foster children."

"Starting now?" I asked.

"Yes, but it usually takes a few months to match. Don't worry. There are plenty of children who need homes."

THE NEXT day, April 1, I was standing in a hallway, talking to a program coordinator, when the telephone in my office rang. I sprinted across the hall. "County Jail #7. This is Sergeant Paulson."

"It's me," said Brian. "Are you sitting down? Meredith called."

I sat down.

"She wants us to take in triplets."

"Okay… April Fool's?"

"No," he continued, "she's serious. The kids are hard to place because of health issues. The babies were born at thirty-two weeks. None of them weighed more than five pounds."

"Okay, and the good news is…?"

"One of the babies, a boy, has a punctured intestine with a colostomy bag, and is undergoing surgery for repair of a heart valve. All three are hypertonic and medically at risk."

Admittedly, all that might have given the most enthusiastic of prospective parents a moment's pause. But we'd been waiting two years, and worst-case scenarios never fazed us. "How old?" I asked.

"Almost three weeks. Born on March 12."

As a Catholic nerd, I knew that March 12 was the feast of Saint Serafina, the little angel, and I thought it an omen. *Little angels in our lives.* This time, I was the one who paused, but just for a moment. "When does she want an answer?"

"Meredith gave us three hours to decide," Brian answered calmly.

This was stunning. I had seen Brian spend half an hour in a Safeway aisle debating which paper towel was a better buy, and here he was telling me that by mid-afternoon we had to decide on whether to up-end our entire lives, in triplicate no less. Part of me knew that Brian had already decided.

We conference-called Marie, Brian's mother. Marie is a nurse in Maine, not just any nurse, but a colonel in the Air Force Reserve who's on the Maine State Board of Nursing. In her matter-of-fact Nor'easter voice she said, "Premature children exposed to drugs in utero will struggle for years, and, given a schizophrenic mother, they have a strong probability of mental illness. The boy with necrotizing enterocolitis might not live until the end of the week."

"You got anything encouraging to follow that up with?" I asked as I lined up all the pencils on the desk in size order, and then faced all the paperclips the same way.

"Only that you two will always provide the very best for them. You're probably the best chance they've got." Then, with just the barest hint of humor, "It's exactly what the two of you need: more stray puppies."

When people talk about Brian and me as a couple, they say that we collect strays: rescue dogs and people with issues. We'd been at it for about fifteen years at that point, rescuing dogs with heart murmurs and kidney failures, persons dying from AIDS, actors who just needed a big break, crystal meth addicts detoxing on our couch and, once, a runaway clown. When we packed up a rental truck and moved to California, the cab was filled with the two of us, two adult dogs and six puppies. We found a home for every puppy.

If we had a working philosophy behind all this, it would be to help those in need. Brian was always helping someone else at an audition get the part that he wanted. And I make a lousy cop because I always feel sorry for both the victim and the perp. Hence the available triplets seemed perfectly suited for our brand of compassion. Not that we were saints. On the contrary, we were scandalous sinners. He drank too much; I ate too much. He smoked too much and if I'd lived in Vegas I would have lost the house. But we did damage only to ourselves, never others. So it came down to the fact that while triplets would be an immense challenge, and we did not want a baby to die on our watch, we weren't doing this for ourselves. We were doing it for the children.

I called Meredith back at one minute before three. "Yes."

"Yes, you'll do it? I need to be completely honest about the boy with the heart surgery and the NEC. No one knows if he will make it."

"We'll do it."

"This is foster parenting with an adoption track, meaning that if no member of the birth mother's family comes forward, you can adopt the triplets."

"What about the birth mother?" I asked.

"I would rule her out completely. She walked out on them in the hospital. Severe schizophrenic, ineligible to parent. She already had one kid removed from her care."

"I'm sorry to hear that."

"That's what foster care is about. You better think up some names. Listen," she continued, "go to Alta Bates Hospital tonight to pick up two of the three triplets."

"And the third?"

"Intensive care at Children's Hospital. We don't know what's going to happen."

Brian was teaching that afternoon. I said to my boss, Captain Amada, "I'm taking the rest of the week off. I'm having a baby tonight. Make that three."

Captain Amada looked up from an incident report. "You might want to consider a leave. But if anyone can do this, it's you."

When I left work, I drove to Target, grabbed a shopping cart, and threw in three of whatever had the word "Baby" on it. Our little compact car was stuffed. I picked Brian up at the Odd Fellows Building in downtown San Francisco, and we started rolling toward I-80.

CHAPTER 2

It Takes Three Villages

"You ready to do this?" Brian asked as we crawled onto the Bay Bridge.

"No," I admitted, "but then it's not like we had nine months to prepare ourselves. What does Tim always say?"

"Leap! And the net will appear!" Tim was Wiccan, and believed in the magic of the universe. For him, the phrase usually meant having sex with the wrong stranger. Whenever he said it to me, I found myself getting a tattoo, skydiving, or climbing a pyramid.

That drive began our transition into parenting: I had been playing KOIT, a soft rock channel, and Brian switched the station to KDFC, classical music. "I've read that it helps stimulate their minds," he explained. This was the first of the countless little changes in routine that would add up to a new way of life.

Around eight o'clock, we parked the car in the lot of Alta Bates Hospital. After finding the neonatal ward, I enthusiastically said to the nurse in charge, "Hi! We're the foster dads!" Maybe a little too enthusiastically.

"How many children have you fostered before?" the nurse asked.

"None."

"When was the last time that you were close to a child?"

"Well, about forty years ago. I used to be a baby, you see."

"So we'll take this slowly," she said with a smile.

Then came the moment: the nurse walked us into a small hospital room, where we saw two impossibly small infants, each weighing five pounds and wriggling inside a tiny cocoon of pink and pastel blue blanket. I was worried that I wouldn't feel anything since I was not the birth father, but I was wrong: I took one look at two of our three children, and fell in love with each of them, and with Brian again, for being willing to do this with me.

"Would you like to hold one?" the nurse asked.

"Sure… uh, how should I pick her up?"

Taking mercy, she said, "I'm going to teach you a few things about feeding and diapering. Let's start with supporting the head."

She worked us until midnight, diapering and re-diapering, burping and re-burping, until we got it right. Never in our wildest dreams had we imagined triplets. The nurse dimmed the lights in the room. "I'll be back in a few minutes. You two get used to this."

And there in the dim light of monitors and beeps, as we sat during that first feeding, Brian said, "We'll need three names. Do you want to call the girl Vivian [my mother] or Marie [his mother]?"

I'm no fool: "Vivienne Marie. You name one boy, and I'll name the other."

Brian, who was holding the boy at the time, said, "I've always liked Joshua, and he looks like a Joshua. And the other?"

"Kyle Thaddeus." In years to come I would come up with a great explanation of how Kyle got his name, but the truth was that I had just been reading a comic book with Catwoman in it, and everybody knows that Selina Kyle is Catwoman. It could have been worse. The Penguin's real name was Oswald Cobblepot.

But the naming was not yet done. With a new name always comes a magical transformation: "You're the *Daddy*," Brian announced. Joshua, in his arms, wiggled at the idea.

I was momentarily flummoxed, but then jumped in with, "And I dub thee *Papa*." The deal was done. When the nurse returned, I asked, "How is the other boy?"

"He's at Children's Hospital. Nick-U." She fussed with the blankets.

"Nick-U?"

"Neonatal Intensive Care Unit. He's had NEC, necrotizing enterocolitis. Not just a colostomy, but an ileostomy." My face crinkled into a question mark. "A colostomy is the lower intestine. In the ileostomy, the surgeon removed nine centimeters of his small or upper intestine. Which means he can't eat anything. And they also repaired a hole in his heart."

The next morning, I called our friend Jon to tell him what was going down. "Guess what?"

"You're out of work again?"

"Better. Brian and I are parents."

"Not another rescue dog. Isn't there a rule about more than three?"

"Jon, listen. We're foster parents. Of triplets."

Telling one friend at a time was enough, given the amount and complexity of the news we'd eventually deliver to one and all. We had met Jon in the early nineties, soon after we moved to San Francisco, when he was dating my crazy boss in a startup software company. Jon was tall, with wavy blonde hair, and clearly unsuited for my manic-depressive supervisor. The company went belly up within a year (thanks no doubt to my skillful marketing). My boss' relationship with Jon lasted no more than three dates, but in the meantime, we had taught Jon how to play pinochle. So we got to keep him in the divorce. He came to our Oscar parties and our Ornament parties, and somewhere along the line he became family, moving into a house about three blocks up.

Jon took off work and came that afternoon to take pictures as we walked Vivienne and Joshua out of the hospital and into our lives. There was a light mist, unlikely but not unheard of in April, and an honest-to-God rainbow.

When we got home, we started fashioning new routines. Our dancer and cop friends had little useful advice, but we became the darling of the neighbors. There were JJ and Helene, two Polish sisters who were mothers of adult daughters. Helene was a nurse, and the two of them stopped in on their way home. Helene would check their health and vital signs and JJ would bring Papa and me dishes like sauerkraut and mushrooms, which sounds awful, but tastes like heaven. Their next door neighbor Dorla, a widow, came along, and sat in the living room, rocking and rocking Joshua. Down the block lived Tita Ann and Tita Nona, two Filipina women who taught us to swaddle the infants. Lori, the manager of Brian's dance company, ODC/San Francisco, a single woman in her late thirties, found that she liked burping a lot more than she liked booking dance tours. It was kind of like the Visit of the Magi, only with a bigger cast.

Tim, sick as he was, showed up with teddy bears for each of the three. One of the senior deputies I worked with, Mike Gunn, told me his wife had just given up the day care business; they brought diapers, books, a crib, and huge battery-driven rockers. Mike's wife knew all the tricks, like why you put a washcloth on your shoulder when you burp a kid, or which *Little Einstein* DVDs will quiet even a newborn infant.

Jon even bought them Gap outfits in light blue, light pink, and light green. This immediately qualified him for Uncle status.

Uncle Jon studied up on all the pragmatic baby stuff that I neglected to learn, like how you wash the clothes in hot water without any softener, and save all the grocery sacks to double-bag diapers in.

After a little bit of drama, the nurses at the Neonatal Intensive Care Unit let us in for visits with Kyle. We had to scrub up like surgeons, donning gowns before they let us in. And in this little plastic box was the humblest baby I had ever seen. Kyle was on a ventilator, with a tube up his nose, needles in his arms for food and medicine, a blood pressure machine on his other arm, a heart monitor on his toe, and a tube coming out of his stomach, and the belly was crusted in blood. The nurse would only let us touch two gloved fingers to his tiny chest.

After a week of not sleeping, Papa and I got into the routine of baby care: feed the baby, burp the baby, change the baby, put the baby to bed, wash baby's clothes, rinse out baby's bottle, and make more formula, just about in time to start feeding the baby. Oh, and that process was in duplicate. In fact it was in duplicate with a third kid in the hospital, across the bay. I often found that I was still in my bathrobe at three o'clock in the afternoon. The witty gay couple with lots of time for canapés and cocktails had quickly turned into two sleep-deprived, middle-aged men.

There was a tenderness in both of us that surprised me. Like the way that Brian just sat in the rocking chair and rocked whatever baby needed it, sometimes for hours at a time, sometimes humming. Or leaving each other little notes again, like we were young and in love all over. Even just lying on the wooden floor, me calming down Miss Grrrl, while Papa quietly let her subcutaneous fluids soak in (in addition to the medically fragile triplets, we had a Pekingese who had lost a kidney, and her second kidney was failing, so we had to inject her with fluids every day). Or surprising the Nick-U nurses with pepperoni pizza and pie made from scratch.

Maybe that's why gay men adopt, so they don't need to feel so much pressure to be butch.

One of the two of us visited Kyle in the hospital every day. For weeks he couldn't eat or be taken out of his incubator bed surrounded by a clear plastic cube, with two holes in it for people to reach in. When we visited him all we could do was to sit next to the bed and hold his less encumbered hand. There was always a little fear that this night he would not make it, and a little horror at all the blood and scabs. But sandwiched between those two emotions was a love that I did not know I possessed — and the certainty that this child and his siblings were meant to be in our lives, and we in theirs.

On another midnight, the late shift nurse walked up to me. The ward was dark. I was hunched in a plastic chair, sticking my hand into the incubator bed, reading *The Cat in the Hat* to Kyle, with him crying the entire time. The nurse, a Filipina woman in her late forties, patted my shoulder and said, "Have you tried singing?"

"I don't know any children's songs. Nurse Vivian didn't believe in them. I can't remember her ever singing me a lullaby."

"Then sing something you know." Being gay and nerdy, I only ever learned the words to Broadway show tunes and a few TV theme songs. So I reached in the plastic box one more time, put my hand on his chest, and crooned in my bargain basement bass voice, *"Just sit right back and you'll hear a tale, a tale of a fateful trip...."*

Kyle went silent, breathing. Just breathing!

The next morning, when Papa and I traded places, him with Kyle and me with Joshua and Vivienne, I smiled and told my trade secret. "I got him to sleep. After *Gilligan* and a couple other TV tunes, it took me the entire cast album of *My Fair Lady,* but it worked."

Brian scowled. "I don't sing."

I scowled back and said two words: "Ann Murray."

He rolled his eyes and started, *"Can I have this dance for the rest of my life?"* Again, Kyle magically paused in his habitual lament, and just breathed.

That night, the late shift nurse walked in as I was singing, *"You got to have a gimmick if you wanna have a chance."*

She handed me a cup of cocoa and said, "You know, it's not just Kyle. The entire ward calmed down. Sometimes the ward gets like that. One fussy baby amps them all up, but when that baby finds peace…" Kyle didn't exactly look at me as much as he turned his head toward the source of the noise. He went from being the fussiest baby on the ward to the most loved. The nurses, who all thought his dimples were charming, argued about whose turn it was to work with him.

By June, Kyle started feeding on a bottle and was healthy enough to leave the hospital. The only problem was the ileostomy bag. First we had to learn how to change it. That very nice Charge Nurse in the NICU talked us through it: "First you take a wipe, and gently rub away the adhesive around the full ileostomy bag. (Papa took the lead and rubbed off the adhesive). Then you very, very gently ease the bag off, making sure that you don't rip any of the baby's skin. (Again, Papa's delicate fingers slid the pouch away. So far, I was doing a great job of standing by.) Then you take another chemical to wipe off the remaining adhesive." Yellow ooze came out of Kyle's intestine. He screamed and…

I woke up in a chair with that very nice charge nurse patting me with a wet cloth, saying, "People faint from this all the time."

"But I'm the son of a *nurse*," I moaned. In the meantime, Papa prepared the new ileostomy bag, stroked Stomadhesive to Kyle's belly, and pressed the bag in place until it set.

ONCE WE had the basics of colostomy bag changing down, the very nice charge nurse said, "Doctor Butler thinks that Kyle could go home in a week or two."

We walked back to our Ford Escort compact, and Papa abruptly announced, "We'll never fit three car seats in here." We drove across the bridge and stopped at a Saturn dealership. We looked desperate, and a salesman pointed out a huge blue sports utility Saturn Vue in Batman blue. Big and expensive, it had a back seat big enough to fit the triplets and a car loan that we could pay off by the next millennium. This was another big lifestyle change: After all those years of mocking sports utility vehicles, I bought the biggest hunk of engine that I could finance to make sure that I was keeping those kids safe.

Somewhere along the line Papa had given up smoking, and I was putting away a lot less pasta, while burning off calories rocking the children to sleep. And Papa, that man who stood in the Christmas tree lot for an hour and a half vacillating about whether to take the seven-foot Douglas Fir or the six-and-a-half-foot Blue Spruce, had become a decisive father who could pick out a new car in less than forty-five minutes.

The dining room table was now always cluttered with laundry, but we no longer cared if the neighbors saw it. Sometime around dusk, most Saturday nights, Dorla showed up with a bottle of wine and JJ showed up with deviled eggs. JJ would start folding shirts, insisting, "I do this a lot better than I change a colostomy bag."

It takes a village to raise a child, and when you have triplets, it takes three villages. So we taught Uncle Jon, JJ, Dorla, Lori and whoever else we could grab how to change the bag. Unless we sang to him, Kyle screamed through the change. It became a qualification for the neighborhood: if you lived on Winding Way, you had to know how to change an ileostomy bag. Oh, and you had to learn the *Gilligan's Island* theme song.

CHAPTER 3

Reanastomosis

Father's Day, 2003

O UR FIRST Father's Day as not just sons, but fathers. My father was a hero. During World War II, he fought in General Patton's Third Armored Spearhead Tank Division. He outmaneuvered Nazi tanks in the Battle of the Bulge, and he himself shot the lock off one of the concentration camps in Germany.

Now that I had children, I doubted that my own accomplishments measured up. Having been captain of the math team or doing the best Bette Davis impression in the Crocker Amazon was not really all that impressive.

In the past few months, Pop had taught me that heroes do the little things. When I called him and told him that we had taken in triplets, he started sewing. The family tradition, for fifty years, was that my father had cut out felt and sewn beads and sequins on top, and every Paulson had his very own hand-decorated Christmas stocking. But he had macular degeneration by this time, and couldn't see very well, and he'd had several heart attacks. He paid his neighbor to thread needles so that he could sew stockings for the triplets. This nearly blind man stayed up night after night, piecing together three stockings out of felt and beads and sequins because he had sewn one for his wife, each of his three sons, each of his other two grandchildren and even the dog. He was not going to let drug-exposed medically fragile grand-triplets feel left out.

Heroes also make sacrifices, large and small. Pop never went to college himself, but he paid for all three of his sons to go. He climbed up telephone poles and worked twelve hour days so that my brothers and I could have that new baseball, or bicycle, or, in my case, bell bottoms. And it was years before any of us appreciated it.

When he taught me how to play cribbage when I was five, I thought it was just so that my brothers could take my money, but eventually I realized that Pop was teaching me how to count. When he bought me a copy of *Teen Titans #4,* I was too focused on the cool picture of Kid Flash to realize that he was giving me an incentive to read.

Pop taught me that the most important thing that you can do for a child is to pay attention.

I tried to honor that. While Papa was off dancing, I asked JJ to watch the babies, while I drove to Sloat's Garden

Center out in the Sunset. I picked out three California Lilac trees (Ceanothus), one for each of them, and then drove home. The triplets sat in the stroller and cheered me on as we planted one in three corners of the small lot in which the blue bungalow sits on Winding Way, so that when Papa got home he would know that his triplets loved him. I was hoping that Kyle, Joshua and Vivienne would grow up to sit under their shade.

Maureen took a picture of the triplets, with a sign that she had hand-painted: "We love our Dads!" and it became our first Father's Day card. No one got breakfast in bed, but then again, who had time for breakfast?

JULY WAS as cool and snug as it always is in San Francisco. Right before Independence Day, Meredith called to say, "The birth mother asked for visits."

"I thought you said that she walked away from the hospital?"

"She did. But the grandmother is making her do this. Just do it this time. I'm betting she's the type who doesn't show up." And so we drove the duplets (Kyle was not yet up for traveling) to Oakland on a foggy Friday afternoon, sat in a very dusty office, waited, and indeed, she did not show up.

The following Monday, Meredith called. "She said she forgot. Can you make it next Friday?" Again, we drove across the Bay Bridge, and again she did not show up.

Meredith called: "One last try. Look, the lawyers for the county will always, and I mean *always*, argue that the birth mother has to be given every possible opportunity. You need to be aware of that. She's a diagnosed schizophrenic, but a county lawyer will ignore even that."

On the third Friday, after waiting an hour, Meredith left. We started to pack up the diaper bag just as the birth mother walked in the door. She was accompanied by the birth grandmother. "Tell them your name," the grandmother prompted.

"Oh, they don't know? I'm Celestina Cruz, but everybody calls me Cici." Cici was a short heavyset woman with curly hair dyed into a burnt red, which she primped the entire time that she was with us. The babies were asleep. "Well, I came to visit them," she said, and poked at Vivienne.

"Please don't do that," Papa intervened. "She needs her sleep."

When Vivienne still did not wake up, Cici lifted her by the elbow until she cried. Cici yelled, "Does she have to scream like that? I can't take that noise." Vivienne reached for her hair, and Cici swatted her.

Cici walked towards the door. The birth grandmother argued with her in Spanish but I couldn't understand what they were saying. Cici slammed the door on her way out.

I picked Vivienne up and said, "Well, it really is time for us to go. Bridge traffic." The birth grandmother watched us with vacant eyes as we bundled up the babies and headed to the car.

ON AUGUST 10, 2003, I was in the Emergency Room at four in the morning with my son who had complications related to his ileostomy.

How did I get there? A few weeks back, during Kyle's last day in the hospital, that nice charge nurse picked up Joshua. "My gosh," she said, deciding all at once to change his diaper, "he has a hernia." I have no idea how you can figure that out in one change of a diaper, but then again, I'm not a nurse.

We took Joshua to meet Dr. Butler, the woman who had originally sliced up Kyle's intestines while simul-taneously sewing up his heart valve. She turned out to be fun and hip, a brown-haired intense woman with glasses. "When this is all over," she said, "I'll watch the trips for a night, while you guys go out for a drink. But right now, Joshua needs this inguinal hernia repaired, and it's time for a reanastomosis."

Blank stares from Papa and me. She continued, "It's time to try sewing Kyle's intestines together."

Papa said, "Can you do both on the same day? Maybe we can save on the Valium." She smiled and nodded and told the calendar nurse to give us a two-for-one special.

The calendar nurse handed me two appointment cards for surgery on August 14th. In the meantime, we got around to the business of caring for triplets.

IN AUGUST, I had gone back to work after taking a few months off, and so we hired a babysitter to watch the babies during the day. The Friday before the scheduled surgery, our babysitter called me at work. "Kyle is fussy and running a temperature."

"I'll come right home." I was scheduled to bring Vivienne and Joshua to see their birth mother again. I got to the bungalow and, sure enough, he was over 101 degrees.

I called our pediatrician, Doctor Halberg, and she said, "Bring Kyle in immediately. But the clinic closes at five." I called Meredith to cancel the visit with the birth mother and gentled him into the car. Racing across 280 and 80 and then the bridge, I made it to the clinic with two minutes to spare. Thanks to the air conditioning of the Vue, Kyle's temperature was below 100 degrees by the time we got to the hospital.

Doctor Halberg fussed over Kyle, and sent me home saying, "Take his temperature every six hours. If it goes over 102, take him to the emergency room immediately." Papa was always pragmatic in these situations, and I was a victim of my own OCD. I saw the worst outcome in everything, and worried about each degree. At eleven o'clock that night it was just below 101, but he was fine by the next morning. By eleven o'clock, his temperature was below 100. At five in the afternoon it was still down and he was charming, which is what we called him when he didn't scream as we fed the other two. Of course, at eleven o'clock that night, his temperature shot up to 102. We called the Advice Nurse on the telephone who said, "Get to a hospital right now!"

But the Advice Nurse had a vastly different sense of urgency than the emergency room staff. I drove to Oakland in eighteen minutes and ran into the ER only to face a bored yawn at the front desk. The receptionist filled out a sheet of paper and told me to join the other ten parents with feverish babies in the waiting room. Kyle's ileostomy was not getting him front row treatment.

Kyle was stubborn. His newest game was called "Don't Let Daddy Sit Down." He smiled and cooed when I stood up and held him. He bellowed in agony when I had the audacity to rest my bottom (yes, I called it *bottom*…even vocabulary changes with children). At home, far from the eyes of social workers, he would play the game for a few minutes and then fall asleep. But not in the ER. I sat down; Kyle howled at a pitch and volume that would shame a tenor at the Met. I stood up; he cried. I walked him; he cried. I even pulled out Mr. Binky, but he still cried.

By this time, his crying had roused the rest of the febrile Emergency Room babies into sympathetic sobbing.

As always, the only thing that quieted him was to walk up and down the hallway singing. Other five-month-old babies liked Barney theme songs and *Twinkle Twinkle*, but not Kyle. He was not happy until I sang, *"You'll be swell. You'll be great,"* from *Gypsy*. He shut up immediately. Realizing that the twilight howl had ceased, the other babies stopped their own crying and opted instead to stare at me. I had no choice but to belt out, *"Gonna have the whole world on a plate. Starting here. Starting now..."* Three hours later, after running through *My Fair Lady, Mame, Annie, Annie Get Your Gun,* and even a little Sondheim, the doctor called Kyle into the examination room. The other mothers applauded, though I'm not sure whether it was an expression of appreciation or relief.

The doctors poked and prodded. I thought that, what with the ileostomy bag and all, I had gotten pretty tough in the past few months. Yet when the nurse walked up to me and said, "The doctor needs to run a catheter tube for a urine sample," I sat down to watch and woke up twenty minutes later.

When I came to, the nurse smiled the serious smile of the business and said, "The test results should be back in an hour."

Two and a half hours later, the night doctor said, "Kyle

has a urinary tract infection and needs to be admitted." This was pretty minor in comparison to his ileostomy and early drug exposure. The doctor continued, "Uncircumcised boy babies get these frequently." As luck would have it, Papa and I were as unfamiliar with uncircumcised boy babies as we were with Vivienne's yeast infections.

The nurse smiled again, her smile saying that *we're all tired*, and informed us the ward would have a bed ready in about half an hour. In real time, that translated to three hours. The waiting room was dim and uncomfortable. Someone had turned the air conditioning up, which meant that we were both cold. The nurse came back with a warmed blanket and wrapped it around Kyle. I sat in a plastic chair and waited, wondering who was awake in the East Bay that I might borrow a sweater from.

At six-thirty, we were given a room. This room was already occupied by another baby and his sleeping mother. After settling Kyle down, I took a nap on the other couch. At about eight in the morning, a nurse came in to do rounds, waking both of us. Susan, the other parent in the room, introduced herself. "This is my son, Jerrell. He has cerebral palsy and he's blind and confined to a wheelchair. He has a cleft palate and has to be fed through a GI feeding tube." She walked around his bed, fussing over the blankets. "I have to stick a tube in his mouth to suck the phlegm out when he gets a cold."

"How hard this must be on your family," I said.

She sighed, and I could see how much effort it was taking her to smile. "I have another son at home but my husband left. He just couldn't take Jerrell. It's funny, with my first son, all I could think of was when I could get him out of diapers. Jerrell will be in diapers for life."

I realized then that I was a lucky man.

Kyle's infection diminished a few mornings later but they kept him in the hospital until the big surgery. Which meant they kept me in the hospital. On the evening of August 13th, Papa and I changed the ileostomy bag for the very last time. Uncle Tim came to watch the last change, commenting, "As a gay foster father, you *had* to get this operation done. It's a question of accessories. He'll be walking soon and wherever would you find the shoes to match the bag?"

But it felt strange to look at the end of his intestines protruding from his little body and think *My God, we have kept these three kids alive against all odds, and tomorrow, for the first time in five months, this kid is actually gonna be able to digest food like the rest of us.*

Papa spent the night in Children's Hospital with Kyle and I slept at Winding Way with Joshua and Vivienne. Uncle Tim stayed in the spare bedroom, saying, "Doesn't matter how sick I am. I can handle the uniplet until Dorla gets here."

At four o'clock in the morning, I woke up and packed up Joshua for his surgery at six. Somewhere on the East Coast, Pop was already praying the rosary for the operation. God bless Dorla, who showed up at four-thirty with a cup of coffee in her hand, and a long day of watching Vivienne ahead of her. Joshua and I drove the Saturn Vue back to Children's Hospital. Kyle, who was getting sedated in the morning, was to begin his surgery at nine-thirty. It was estimated that his surgery, which involved finding the other end of the intestine and then attaching it, was going to take at least four hours.

The no-nonsense nurse in Doctor Butler's office told me to be there by six-thirty. The even more no-nonsense nurse in pre-operative surgery told me to be there by six. I must have looked like a shiftless-no-account-foster-dad-who-never-shows-up-for-surgery-on-time kind of guy. We got there at five forty-five. I sat there from five forty-five until seven forty-five without so much as a cup of decaf. It was worse for Joshua, because he hadn't even had a cup of Enfamil. He howled, which woke up every baby in Children's Hospital, and may well have been heard across the bay. Finally, the anesthesiologist stepped out of the operating room and said, "Well, his lungs work. Let's get to the other parts."

The nurse who hadn't trusted my punctuality gave me a pager and said, "We will return a healthy baby to you in two hours." I went up to the fourth floor, where Kyle was busy convincing the nurses that not only had he not eaten since the night before, but that we had never fed him at all. After two hours of me reading comic books while Papa read a Mercedes Lackey novel, another nurse came in and announced, "We're ready for the brother." Kyle gave that pathetic smile that only a child without working intestines can give.

We took the elevator down to the third floor. A very beleaguered nurse looked at Kyle and asked, "Is he as loud as his brother?" Kyle took that opportunity to start whimpering and clawing at the ileostomy bag, convincing her that he was the nice one.

Just then, Doctor Butler walked in, dressed in bright green scrubs with Kermit the Frog and Miss Piggy on them. She crowed, "Joshua's surgery went well. In and out. Ready for Round Two."

"Can you throw in a third surgery for free? I could use a little liposuction."

She shook her head and said, "Kyle's surgery will take about four hours, but sometimes things get complicated and it could take longer. I'll be back by one." With that she headed back to surgery.

The nurse walked us into the recovery room where Papa and I watched Joshua breathe for forty-five minutes before they moved us to Neonatal Intensive Care, our old stomping grounds. Either Papa or I had visited Kyle there every day, and as you may imagine, we'd made a few friends. Wheeling the kid in on a gurney, I felt like Norm walking onto the set of *Cheers*. A social worker whispered, "That's the man who sings the show tunes. He's loud, but not as loud as the baby." Joshua was a hit with the nurses, as they all assumed that he was Kyle and had been miraculously cured of his ileostomy. Each nurse cooed over him, and then the chaplain, and even a doctor or two.

We settled him in, sang *Gilligan's,* and then went down to the cafeteria to grab lunch. Papa ate nothing. After a wilted salad and flat, lukewarm root beer, I went back to the counter to get a cup of decaf, only to learn that they didn't serve decaf. This is just the sort of thing to set off an OCD person while he is waiting for his infant son to have his intestines repaired: *a hospital without decaf!* We walked across the street to find some. By this time it was one-thirty. I did not panic at one-thirty. Papa suggested, "I wish you had a vice like smoking or drinking. Or just caffeine. It really does pass the time more quickly." By two o'clock I was fretting mildly.

At two-thirty, five hours into the surgery, I became concerned. At three o'clock, I became very concerned. At three-thirty, I grabbed the first nurse I saw and demanded some answers.

The beeper, signaling that the surgery was over,

didn't go off until 4:02 PM. Papa and I hustled back to the recovery room. Doctor Butler gave us the thumbs-up sign. Kyle was connected to seven different tubes with all sorts of beepers and alarms. What I thought was a simple matter of sewing one end of an intestine back to the other end of an intestine was actually much more complicated.

Doctor Butler explained: "Because Kyle had a disease of the bowel, I had to open the cavity, remove the intestines and check every single centimeter of the intestine to inspect it for scarring and strictures. It's like opening a can of Chef Boyardee, putting it on the table, laying out each strand of spaghetti end to end, cutting out the broken pieces, sewing the strands back together again, and fitting them back in the can. I then closed the can and made it look like I'd never been there."

Papa added, "Like Ginger Rogers doing everything Fred Astaire did. Backwards in high heels."

She continued, "I actually removed very little of his intestines and I expect a full recovery, but we won't start him on food for a few days."

"Oh, joy," I sighed. "Another dissatisfied baby."

Doctor Butler said, "His intestines were too swollen to be tested at this point, but in about three days he can start eating food again. In the meantime, we'll feed him intravenously. But," she smiled mischievously, "I listened to what you said about having the third operation for free, so I threw in an appendectomy."

"You took out his appendix?!" Papa was appalled.

"Well, it's not like he needs it."

"Well, Doctor," Papa replied with his stiff New England smile, "Thank God you didn't remove any other organs he isn't using right now. I want to be a grandfather someday. But everything is all right now?"

Doctor Butler smiled hesitantly. "My main worry throughout the course of these months since his initial surgery was that the intestinal tract might not work. Now we have removed about eight centimeters of ileum and I am just a little worried that that there might be perforations that we haven't seen."

"So let me get this straight," I inquired. "We still don't know whether food will actually go down the esophagus, through the stomach, through the small intestine, through the large intestine and out the back door?"

"No, but we've got a lot better shot at it than we ever did before."

"How will we know?"

"Well, to quote you, when you see something come out the back door."

An hour later, we wheeled Kyle back to the Neonatal Intensive Care Unit. Doctor Butler smiled and said, "Now you can start sleeping through the night."

Of course, Joshua chose that moment to start teething.

FIVE DAYS later, after I walked the dogs, got in the car and drove across the bridge, I settled in the Neonatal Intensive Care Room with my morning decaf and I smelled poop. This would not be unusual at home. Despite all our best efforts, Miss Grrrl and Wolfcub pooped always about a minute before their walk time. Joshua and Vivienne pooped three minutes after I had just changed their diapers.

But this poop was a brand new smell, here in the Nick-U. I put down my paper cup, and turned to see Kyle in the corner crib, smiling like he had just won at *Jeopardy*. The back door worked!

Yet scarring could still occur in the intestinal tract, meaning that we were not yet out of the woods. Kyle had been on morphine, which is not great for any baby, let alone a baby whose birth mother took Haldol, alcohol, and cocaine while pregnant, a combination I do not even recommend for my brother Earl, the family expert on pharmaceutical mixing. In addition, Kyle was still hypertonic, and the fact that his birth mother was schizophrenic gave him about a thirteen percent shot at it himself. Multiply that fact times the triplets, and we had about a fifty/fifty chance of schizophrenia in the family.

But Kyle had pooped, and for the day, pooping was a victory. He smiled at me all morning, and, I daresay, he was quite proud of what he'd voided. In the grand scheme of things, his poop was minor and inconsequential compared to his sister Vivienne, who had made pooping into a fine art. Not only was her volume much greater than you could imagine would be produced by a five-month-old baby, but her timing was exquisite. You could change her diaper fifteen times, but put that baby into a closed car and she would instantly mix up and deliver a brew that would put a sailor to shame.

Today had been a good day. It meant that we had a shot at a normal life. The box score for the Fisher-Paulsons read as follows: two relatively healthy premature infants, one infant on the way to relatively healthy, two dogs on the decline, and one dog as healthy as a puppy (Diva). There was even hope for me to reduce my cholesterol count.

As I am the type of person who is always worrying at his own happiness, I called Uncle Tim. This was typical of how I used the precious moments each day when I could actually dial the telephone: I'd call Uncle Jon when I wanted to figure out how to wire a baby monitor, and I'd call Uncle Tim when I wanted to figure out how life worked. It's the Irish in me, with a gay twist. In lieu of the parish priest, I consulted with the local Wiccan high priestess.

"Hello?" came his distracted voice.

"Hello back, Uncle Tim."

"Not that I don't love your small talk, but you sound like you have a Zen question today."

"We saw Doctor Halberg today. Even the nurse said it was a miracle how much the triplets have grown, how they have changed. What are the chances for normal?"

I could hear the sound of Tim working his way through kitchen drawers, looking for a lighter no doubt. "Normal is overrated. And the miracle is not that the babies have changed. It's that *you* have." A pause, as, undoubtedly he had found the missing lighter. "You and Brian. A year ago, your biggest worry was what appetizers to make for the Oscar party and now" — the cigarette lighter clicked — "now, you're getting hernias repaired and intestines sewn together, and you don't even blink."

"I'm terrified."

"You're terrifying. Love has changed you. Nothing fazes you anymore. Enjoy today, if for no other reason than the fact that your youngest son can poop."

BRIAN'S MOTHER, Marie, was now *Nana,* and Nana was fierce. Her first husband, Brian's father, had left her in North Monmouth, Maine to raise the boys alone when Brian was ten. As a single mother, she'd managed to raise two sons while working full time as a nurse and serving in the Air Force Reserve on weekends. Even with all that, she never missed any of Brian's gymnastic meets or Craig's basketball games. Between Nana and Nurse Vivian, we had a lot to live up to if we intended to be good parents.

Nana flew across the country to bring some sanity to the blue bungalow of bedlam. Quiet, calm and firm, she did not tell me that I was holding the baby all wrong, but she did teach me in a no-nonsense way, "Test the formula on your wrist. Your wrist will know what a baby wants. As she drinks, hold her head up high enough to let gravity help you." In two days I was a pro.

One afternoon she went with Papa to the hospital to visit Kyle, to inspect how well the doctors had been performing their work. She had been facing down doctors and generals and senators all her life. I was sure that she would keep those pediatricians in line. This left me alone with the duplets. I rushed through cleaning the bathroom and brushing out the dogs and giving Miss Grrrl her kidney medicine. By then Vivienne was bellowing for her bottle.

Vivienne, ever the sommelier, had become a connoisseur of formula. Enfamil was the infant equivalent of Pouilly Fuisse '57. She licked the nipple, sniffed the bouquet and slowly sipped her bottle. Some fifty-five minutes later, my arm had gone to sleep supporting her head while she savored the dregs. Joshua, who decided that I had not paid enough attention to his teething gums, snorted.

It was a cool sunset in San Francisco and the dusk was gathering fog around its edges. There were no lights on in our blue bungalow and there was nothing I could do to make Vivienne drink faster. There was nothing I could do to make Joshua go back to sleep. The only thing I could do was sit there and pat Vivienne's back. Diva curled up on my feet. As the evening shadows grew, I picked up Joshua and rocked him and said, "This too will pass. Some day, when you are my age, you'll worry more about teeth exiting than teeth entering."

A foghorn sounded from way across the city, muffled by the very fog it warned about, and as the twilight grew dark, Joshua's lids grew heavy and his head slipped onto my chest. His breathing grew longer and he smiled in early sleep. As the three of us sat there in our quiet contentment, I thought about how I had spent my life rushing. I was learning that on some days, you cannot rush the moment. Some days the moment has to come to you.

CHAPTER 4

The Passing of a Diva

"A Pekingese is not a pet dog. He is an under-sized lion."
—A.A. MILNE

August 23, 2003

THE WORLD is divided into Those Who Love Dogs and Those Who Don't. Donald, my older brother, made no secret of the fact that he Did Not Like Dogs. When I was fourteen, I found this stray we named Whiskers. Or rather he found me, as he appeared crawling out of the pine woods that still grew then in Yaphank, New York. Whiskers was part terrier and part leftover hound, scratched-up and mangy. Donald, who had moved out of the house by then, gravely warned, "If you let Kevin start taking in strays now, what will happen when he starts dating?"

Donald was jealous that I kept Whiskers, or that Whiskers kept me. Even thirty years later, when his second wife and children convinced him to bring Phoebe, another stray, into *their* home, he did so reluctantly, muttering, "We're getting to be as bad as Kevin."

But Papa and I were Dog Lovers. Thirteen years before this tale began, Miss Grrrrl had moved in with us. Papa had given up smoking, and as a reward, I let him have the dog who desperately needed a home, this dog that he had wanted since the day we met.

We have lived with Pekingeses ever since. Less than a year later, we met Diva. She was a lonely-looking blonde Pekingese, moping in a cage in a pet store. At the time, I wasn't sure that I wanted a second dog, since Miss Grrrrl was such a handful, and this was, after all a *pet store* dog, but Papa was still not smoking and my friend Amanda convinced me, saying, "After all, that dog is such a splendid Diva, how could you not love her?" But being a pet store dog, it turned out that Diva was the only pedigree in the family.

The third dog? For reasons I don't entirely understand, I gave in when Papa said, "Why don't we breed Miss Grrrrl?" Papa was still not smoking at the time, and was not gainfully employed, so I figured that he had the free time to manage all this, and I was always willing to give him something to do besides smoke. A friend of ours drove us to a suburban home in New Jersey, where a Pekingese stud lived. The Vice President of the Northeastern States

Pekingese Club, a woman with perfectly styled gray hair and a Donna Karan dress, took one look at Miss Grrrl and asked, "Are you sure you want to breed this… bitch?"

"Lady, I replied, "I am paying you three hundred dollars for your stud, and believe-you-me that is more than I have ever paid for sex. So let's just do this."

I picked my dog up a day later. The stud lay panting on the porch, exhausted. The Vice President, no longer perfectly coiffed, looking as worse for wear as the stud (who would have thought that watching two Pekes do it would be this exhausting?) said, "In all my years of breeding, I have never seen a bitch with such… enthusiasm." And Miss Grrrl? She just smiled.

A few weeks later, Miss Grrrrl bore six beautiful puppies, the last of which we called Wolfcub. This was the week that I quit my job, and we rented a truck and drove to California. We were kind of like Johnny Appleseed, only with Pekingeses. Everywhere we stopped, someone fell in love with a puppy and a Peke found a home. But we kept the runt of the litter, unadoptable because of luxotic elbows, our little Wolfcub.

We began our lives in San Francisco walking those three dogs around the block on Fair Oaks Street. True story: the first person we ever met while walking the dogs was the author Armistead Maupin, whose iconic *Tales of the City* had drawn our hearts to San Francisco. Miss

Grrrrl and Wolfcub loved walks but Diva hated them. She liked nothing more than a warm cushion and a piece of chicken. Or carrot. She was the only dog I have met who ate raw potatoes.

Diva was always the sweet dog. Miss Grrrrl barked at Rottweilers and Wolfcub strutted in front of Doberman Pinschers, but Diva always walked behind the other two, anxious to finish up her outing and get back to her nap with as little fuss as possible. She never snarled at either dog, even when they were eating her fair share of cheeseburgers. She never barked or growled when we dressed her up in a tutu or angel's wings or a Superdog costume, for that matter. When she really wanted something, she reared up on her hind legs and batted her front paws. And what she really wanted most was for someone to scratch her right behind the ears.

YOU NEVER know when certain moments are going to be the last. Two years before the triplets became the center of our universe, Nurse Vivian and Pop had come out for Thanksgiving dinner. Nurse Vivian loved the blue bungalow. She said to me, "This reminds me of my own Grandmother's house. All on one floor and all so sweet. The only thing you really need to make it perfect is a kitchen table."

"Why a kitchen table?"

"Because that is where you build a family. This is the kind of home," she said, "where you sit around the kitchen table drinking coffee and planning the day, where you play cards at night, or sip a glass of wine at one in the morning. The heart of this house is the kitchen."

Nurse Vivian loved cooking for Thanksgiving. She and I both got up at four-thirty that morning to start the meal. While I heated up the oven, she untrussed and retrussed the Butterball turkey. I set the sausage to sizzling, and Nurse Vivian sautéed the onions and celery. As I was chopping up the fresh sage, she winced. "You're putting sage into MY stuffing?" she wailed. "You ate my stuffing for forty years without complaining, and now you're putting *plants* in it?"

We quibbled about the peeling of the potatoes, and whether yams were really necessary, but I did find out why her gravy was so smooth.

But dinner was a success, and even Pop ate the plants in the stuffing. Dinner was followed by my mother's apple pie, which was, is, and will always be the best pie in the entire world. Here was the odd thing: she slipped the recipe card out of her purse and handed it to me. She had, at one time, typed all of her recipes onto the back of penny postcards, and those cards were guarded ferociously.

"How about the one for lemon meringue?" I begged. "I never get the eggs white to rise like yours."

"Some secrets can never be told," she smiled.

After the neighbors left, we played bridge. This was a rite of passage in the Paulson family. Daughters-in-law were not fully accepted until they learned the difference between a major suit and a minor suit, a small slam and a grand slam. Playing bridge with us was the closest that Nurse Vivian and Pop would ever be to accepting gay marriage.

Bridge is divided up into little games, called rubbers (and, Pop, being Catholic, never explained the derivation of the term). But I stumbled through the first rubber, while Brian proved a surprise. He counted each card, calculated each play, and by the time that he finessed a small slam, he had out-muscled my sister-in-law Christine in the hierarchy of out-laws.

The next day, we watched Papa dance the lead role (the Boy) in the ODC/San Francisco production of *The Velveteen Rabbit*. Pop and Nurse Vivian had only seen Brian play backup dancer to the likes of Neil Diamond or John Davidson, so it was nice for them to see him up front on stage, moving to the gentle harp music of Benjamin Britten. We went out to Yet Wah's afterward. Pop ordered Sweet and Sour Shrimp because despite whatever the new-fangled Pope said, Catholics don't eat meat on Friday.

Nurse Vivian and Pop stayed only three days because, as she said, "Guests are like fish. After three days they begin to stink." On Saturday morning, she got dressed, packed her suitcases, and made her breakfast, which had been a soft-boiled egg for more than fifty years. She picked up the dishes, and washed them in the sink, saying to Pop, "Time to go."

"But we've got plenty of time," I protested. "Your flight isn't for another four hours. I can make it to SFO in twenty minutes."

She picked up her battered green vinyl suitcase. "Harold, put your jacket on. No one ever really knows how much time they have."

"What does *that* mean?" I asked, feeling troubled as I took my last swig of decaf.

"Well, we're all getting old. This is probably the last trip that I'll ever make out here."

I didn't believe her, joking, "Oh, Nurse Vivian, you have to come out next year. I still haven't learned how to make your meringue."

Nurse Vivian said, "Sometimes you just know when something is for the last time." What could I say to that? We walked to the Batman-blue Ford Escort under the olive trees we had planted a few months earlier. It was Nurse Vivian who had suggested those trees, and prompted me to organize a planting with the Friends of the Urban Forest. She smiled as she plucked a leaf. "You know, the Greeks used olive branches when they wanted peace," and she got in the car. Pop sat in the backseat, and turned down his hearing aid.

In the car, as we drove down Bayshore, I casually said, "Brian and I are thinking about adopting."

"You have enough dogs!" Nurse Vivian exclaimed. "What you need is a kitchen table."

"I mean children," I offered, speeding up to get onto 101 South.

Fortunately, my father was nearly deaf and so could hear none of this conversation. But I could feel my mother's eyes rolling from the passenger seat. "Two middle-aged men playing house. Take a vacation instead. Buy a fancy car. Less heartbreak."

As we arrived at the airport, she insisted, "Drop us off here at the door."

"No, parking is right over there," I said, pointing to the short term lot.

"Do you know how much parking costs?" she challenged. And there was no arguing with her. I stopped the car at the curb, got the suitcase out of the trunk, and hugged my father. Then I kissed Nurse Vivian and she said, "Remember our mutual friend," picked up her suitcase, and walked into the terminal.

When I got home, I went to strip the bed in the guest bedroom, as she had taught me. Nurse Vivian had left the top drawer of the dresser open, which was very unusual for her. I opened the drawer and found that she had left the statue of St. Jude Thaddeus, "our mutual friend," wrapped in tissue paper.

This was the statue that she had bought when she was pregnant with me. We didn't have furniture in the living room in South Ozone Park. In 1956, Nurse Vivian told the neighbors that we were painting, and she promptly set up a stepladder with a roller and brush. In 1963, the stepladder was still up, because we still had no living room furniture. But we did have a dining room table, that blonde bleached wood so popular in the fifties, and a matching china cabinet. On the second shelf of the china cabinet, exactly in the middle, stood the statue of Saint Jude Thaddeus.

Saint Jude was the Paulson family saint — the patron saint of the impossible. All three of Nurse Vivian's sons were impossible, but especially me. Nurse Vivian had Earl and Donald within two years of each other, but then had five miscarriages. On her eighth pregnancy, she prayed a novena to Saint Jude that she would have a healthy baby girl. Nine months later, Saint Jude delivered me.

Saint Jude watched over the family meals every night at 5:30 pm when Pop got home from work at Ma Bell, after ten hours of climbing telephone poles. Saint Jude watched over all of the homework ever finished at that dining room table, from the spelling of "cat" to the Cartesian plane.

Saint Jude watched as the neighbors came over to play penny poker, the Widow Sally and the Widower Joe, and every time that Nurse Vivian won a round, she would smile at Pop and say, "Saint Jude is the patron saint of the inside straight."

And Pop would ask, "Did you read that in Hoyle?"

We lived under the flight path of Idlewild (later Kennedy) Airport, and so there was a lot of shaking and vibrating of that china cabinet. But if Saint Jude ever turned around completely, Nurse Vivian would insist that a death had just come. And somehow always it did. It may have been the neighbor's hamster, but a death always occurred.

Nurse Vivian passed away the May after that Thanksgiving visit, succumbing to ovarian cancer, the silent killer. There's a part of me that never gets away from that loss, that always wants to call her up and ask her whether it was basil or parsley she put in her meatballs. I wondered if Vivienne would grow up with any resonance with the Grandmother we named her after.

Vivienne Marie: two fierce women to live up to.

But this chapter is not about Nurse Vivian or Vivienne, it is about one day in August 2003. While the babies slept, I got ready to take the long-neglected hounds for a walk. Just as I had done for the past thirteen years, I harnessed up Miss Grrrl and Wolfcub, who were both always eager to walk. I then put the harness around Diva, who would have liked to sleep for another few minutes. We walked up the block and back, and when we came in the house, I gave them their morning pills as I usually did. For no particular reason, I fixed them each a fresh bowl of wet dog food and rice, one of their favorite treats. I wish that I had known it would be Diva's last.

Papa and I went to the hospital and visited Kyle and when we came back at around six o'clock, I again harnessed up Miss Grrrrl, got Wolfcub ready, and put the harness around Diva. But this time, Diva refused to stand. I coaxed her for a bit but she still wouldn't stand. Papa and I looked at each other.

"You watch the kids," I said. I picked her up, carried her to the car and drove to All Animals Emergency Hospital where the doctor, a calm Indian woman with glasses, did an examination. She took her to another room for an x-ray. When she walked back into the waiting room, I knew. She said quietly, "Dogs get hurt sometimes. Jumping off the couch. Down the stairs. We don't know what. But her spine is ruptured. That heat you feel on her back? That's pain. It will only get worse."

"Surgery?"

She shook her head, "Not at this point. If it was me, I would… euthanize her. But it's your choice."

I debated whether or not to call Papa. And then Diva whined, and I thought that I didn't really want to ask Papa whether or not to put her down. Only one of us should bear that. So there I stood, holding her, as the very nice doctor injected an anesthetic that put our Diva to sleep forever. She blinked, once, and was gone.

Everything fell apart inside. I cried and cried, and the doctor walked me outside. A receptionist asked, "Do you want her cremated?" I still couldn't form words, but nodded, and I signed papers, and picked up the empty leash and walked back to the car.

Wouldn't it be great if we remembered to tell people that we love them? I can't help but wish that I had always given Diva extra chicken.

I was very glad for the thirteen years with her. She taught me, as no one else has, that you can do all the wagging and chasing that you want in this life, but nothing is quite as satisfying as curling up with someone you love in your lap.

Kevin Fisher-Paulson

CHAPTER 5

Not Sitting on the Dock of the Bay

Labor Day Weekend 2003

THE BLUE bungalow was in tumult after Diva's passing. Miss Grrrl, the alpha, wandered around the
house looking lost. She gave me confused glances when
I took her out for walks. She had spent thirteen years herd-
ing Diva, walking a little bit faster than her, making sure
she stayed in line… and here she was with no one to boss
around.

And what of the only other girl — Vivienne, the alpha
baby? She was missing Kyle as she had only one brother
to boss around. On Friday she and Joshua had gotten
vaccinations, and that gave them an excuse for being
cranky. Vivienne milked that crankiness for a good three
days. She cried when I fed her. She cried when I burped
her. She cried when I put her down. I'm not good with
crying, but it was hard to make that clear to a six-month-

61

old. And she let me know that she resented every trip I took to the hospital for Kyle.

Kyle was improving. He pooped more and more, and had gotten his first diaper rash. Who would have thought that diaper rash was a sign of progress? But it was always one step forward and two steps back; the next day he failed the audiology test.

We had an appointment to take Vivienne to meet with the birth mother. We drove across the bridge to Oakland, and we waited. Meredith waited. Cici arrived half an hour late, clutching two Big Gulps, saying, "I stopped to get soda for Poppy."

"These babies are still drinking formula," Papa said calmly.

"At what age do you give them soda?" She picked up Vivienne, who started crying. "This one never shuts up. I couldn't stand it. That's why I called her Poppy.""

Cici had given them the names Poppy, Seamus and Angel. Meredith had told us to use our own names, but I did want to acknowledge the history, so I asked, "Who were they named after?"

"Oh, Poppy, 'cause poppies make you sleep, and Seamus 'cause of this guy I slept with and Angel 'cause I like doing Angel Dust. I mean I used to. Would it be better if I brought diet soda?" Vivienne cried, and Cici huffed with exasperation every time.

Meredith had been tutoring Cici on how to hold the baby, but it seemed that every time Cici handled a baby, the baby cried. Meredith quietly said, "Cici, you need to cut your nails before you see the babies again. The way you pick them up, you keep scratching them."

Cici looked down at her manicured nails and shook her head. Mercifully, the visit ended.

We drove back towards the bridge in the Saturn Vue. "Well?" I asked.

"Well what?"

"What do you think?"

"I think that I'm afraid to think about it," Papa sighed. He turned the radio to KDFC. Pavanne for a Dead Princess. "I wish I liked her. I wish I thought she liked the children, at least. But…" his voice trailed off.

"But what?" I slowed down as we reached the toll booth, grabbed for my wallet, gave the attendant the fee.

Brian watched all this before answering, "But it's like a game to her. Like these aren't children. They're dolls. And her mother told her to get her dolls back. She doesn't look at us like we're people. She looks at us like we're the hired help."

We drove across the bridge. Brian finished: "And it *is* a game to her. She's acting normal till she gets what she wants. I am more worried than I have ever been."

We drove south on 280, took the Geneva/Ocean

Exit, and drove across Geneva until we reached the blue bungalow. Vivienne woke up as I turned off the engine. "Pretty girl," I said and she smiled at me. "You're definitely not the kind of poppy that makes *me* sleep."

I HAD taken a leave of absence for a few weeks from work for the surgery, and it was time to go back. But I had not been on vacation; I had been in a hospital with about two hundred different diseases floating about. So, on my first day back at the jail, the stomach flu hit. It wasn't one of those minor inconveniences, like a little gas, but a full-blown stomach flu, complete with nausea, vomiting, diarrhea, and even more than my usual crankiness.

By the time I got home, I couldn't even feed the duplets. Between trips to the bathroom, I dialed Uncle Jon and Aunt Lori, who took turns watching the kids all night. Even Uncle Tim spent an hour with them.

In the morning, after a long night in the bathroom, all news became good news. I felt better. Papa and I went to the hospital, and the nurse told us that Kyle now weighed a whopping eleven pounds, and that all of the IV drips and blood lines and blood pressure monitors and heart monitors had been removed and he was free to leave the hospital.

We then stood through a half hour lecture on bottom care. Who knew that taking care of a bottom could be so complicated? The nurse offered, "One trick is to use a blow dryer to the buttocks prior to placing the skin protectant. Wash the bottom, after drying spray on Wipe 3M No Sting Film Barrier. Completely cover the diaper with a 50:50 mix of Calmoseptine and Ilex, then on top of that layer, cover the bottom with Stomadhesive powder. Then a layer of Aloe Vera gel with Lidocaine, then a layer of Nystatin prescription. Do *not* use baby wipes. Only cotton squares soaked in baby oil."

This bottom was more complicated to manage than the Starship Enterprise.

When Papa and I first moved the duplets in with us, Uncle Jon brought over a mother of twins. She said, "People always treat mothers of twins like they're famous. Gay foster parents of mixed race triplets will be *rock stars*."

And that is how we felt when we left the hospital: practically famous. The unit doctor came to say goodbye; the developmental specialist came to say goodbye. The audiologist came to say goodbye; the surgeon came to say goodbye. Even the Director of the Intensive Care Unit came to say goodbye. The Director said, "All of us believe that these babies were meant to be raised by you. I do not know how they would have survived without the care you gave."

And then the nurses came to say goodbye, one by one, one of them demanding, "Bring them back for a visit.

They don't even have to be sick." Another nurse cried, saying, "Your babies are the most beautiful babies in the world." She was right, of course. Thank God we hadn't relied on genetics.

We left Children's Hospital Intensive Care Unit for what we hoped was the very last time and drove across the bridge. Kyle smiled his heartbreaker smile at everyone in the blue bungalow. Even Miss Grrrrl wagged her tail. We still missed Diva of course, but we felt like a family again, with all of the triplets exercising their lungs.

Maureen and Dorla came over the following night to rescue us from Parents-of-Triplets Syndrome. Although Maureen expressed great trepidation about changing Kyle's challenging bottom, she bravely said, "Take as long as you want at dinner. Provided that you're back in two hours."

Dorla said nothing, but looked worried and blinked a lot.

We met up with Uncle Jon and Tim, who were delighted to find us outside of Winding Way, eating at Yet Wah's. We had even changed our shirts so that we didn't smell quite so much like formula and baby vomit. Tim said, "You're almost like normal gay men."

"I never knew that normal could be so far away," I said, as Irene brought over a carafe of blush wine and a virgin mai tai for Tim. I raised my glass, "To Diva, and all the other orphans."

"To Diva!" We clinked glasses.

"I think I forgot how to small talk," Brian admitted, stabbing a pot sticker with his chopsticks. "But other than that, this is good, right?" This was a question to Tim. Tim had been our most eccentric friend for years, and despite being bipolar and a Wiccan and a recovering heroin addict, it was his opinion that would always weigh on us most.

Tim just nodded, "The universe provides. These children were meant to be with you, whatever the future brings."

Uncle Jon asked, "Did you just read that out of a fortune cookie?"

"No, I've been saving the line. I know my role. I'm their Greek chorus."

It was great to eat an entire dinner without hearing a baby cry. But also a little eerie. The pot stickers were as delicious as ever, and the nibbles of General Kung Pao chicken that I stole off Brian's plate were wonderful, despite the fact that my chopsticks did not work.

One hour and forty-five minutes later, we drove back, and found that the babies were not only still alive, but quite entertained by their new babysitters. Vivienne had convinced them that we never fed them, and so they each had had about three bottles in the less-than-two-hours we were gone. Miss Grrrl and Wolfcub were wagging their tails, which told me that the babysitters had also found the secret supply of Snausages. And, lo and behold, Maureen discovered that she sang show tunes as well as I did. Of course, that wasn't saying much.

Kyle waited a moment and then whimpered. He had the most pathetic cry of the three, so even though I had learned to ignore Joshua's operatic tenor, and Vivienne's Brobdingnagian yell, it was hard to ignore the boy who could be crying over his reattached bowels or his newly-used bottom or teething, or failing the hearing test, or last month's urinary tract infection. Or, perhaps the boy of a thousand challenges was just learning to enjoy attention. He whined and I picked him up, and all was right with the world.

It was the Sunday afternoon of Labor Day weekend, yet Papa and I were not at the beach soaking up the last of the summer heat. We were not at a barbecue gorging on spare ribs. We were not even at a backyard picnic. We were at home with the loudest triplets God ever created. We were all still in pajamas: Vivienne in her pink baby dolls, Kyle in his Batman blue pajamas, and Joshua in the green velour dragon pajamas that Uncle Craig sent. I was still in my red plaid bathrobe that Amanda had given me during my Noel Coward phase.

You make choices when you get kids. (*You* meaning

me.) Just a year prior to baby rearing, Papa and I actually had some leisure time. The dogs were our most serious responsibility then, so we foisted them off on Uncle Jon, allowing us to fly to Maine for Papa's fortieth birthday. We had a great time at the party, and for the first time in our relationship, with a lot of help from Papa's mother, I actually surprised him (this is why I could never manage an affair). Nana had arranged for a party with friends from all over Papa's life, and while I took him to see *My Big Fat Greek Wedding*, all of them went over to her house. Papa was shocked and it gave him the chance to re-connect with a lot of friends he hadn't seen in years.

The next day, Nana threw the annual family Labor Day party. The Labor Day party and the Christmas tree party are the two big events of the year in Papa's family. Unless you're in the hospital or in a coffin, you don't have a good excuse for not being there. Papa's cousin, Tony, made a chili hotter than your first date in college. Aunt Ellen made lots of high-calorie desserts that are impossible to burn off before Christmas, Papa's favorite being Needhams, a confection of coconut dipped in chocolate. Needhams were usually a Christmas treat but Aunt Ellen made a big batch for Papa on Labor Day as well. Papa would always fly the batch home to San Francisco to put in the freezer, letting himself have only one or two a month until they were gone. Not me. Tim and I could eat the entire tin in a single siege.

A few months before this Labor Day party, we had flown out to Yaphank for Nurse Vivian's funeral service. A whole slew of cousins from both sides of the family came for the typical Irish wake, meaning that we all kept going back to the house for cold cut sandwiches and beer between rosaries. During one of those breaks, I got the whole family to go outside onto the lawn and I took a picture as they stood at the top of the hill. I realized that in the forty-five years that we had all been cousins, we had never taken a family picture together while Nurse Vivian was alive.

On that particular Labor Day I decided that I didn't want the same thing to happen to Papa's family. I borrowed a camera and I told Papa's brother Craig to go out on the dock along with Craig's wife, Lisa, Uncle Roger, Aunt Pat, Aunt Ellen, cousin Tony, cousin Mark, and cousin Cathy. After I had gotten almost everyone together, Nana's husband, Dick, asked, "What are you doing?"

"Oh, I'm getting everybody together for a family picture. I figured it would look great on the dock, with the water, and the lighthouse, and the trees in the background."

Dick, ever the dry Mainer, said, "You do know that is a very small dock, built with only two braces."

Being not very proficient with technical terms and thus

not clear on the mechanics of said braces, I sagely replied, "Well, I better hurry up and take the picture then."

I looked down into the camera view, focused the lens, and just as I snapped the picture, I heard a loud crack. I looked into the camera again, and there was Papa's entire family sliding into Lake Cobbossee. Aunt Patty screamed. Uncle Roger yelled, "Women and children first!" And suddenly we were hauling people out of the water.

As it turns out, the water was only about four feet deep, so there was danger really only to Dick's dock and my reputation. The family took it pretty well, all things considered. Cousin Cathy's husband Leonard said, "Well, thank God you did this. I was always the in-law on the outs. But I could never top this. Not many men try to drown all of their in-laws at the same time."

I never did get a copy of either family picture.

WHEN YOU have kids you give up on nights out at the movies, dinners at the newest restaurants. You find that some of the things you have given up, such as keeping the house clean, were never all that important in the first place. I'd learned that a clean house is not the virtue that I once thought it was. In fact, a neat house will only make you neurotic. You cannot keep a house neat and still raise Pekingeses, who have nothing to do with their time but shed. You cannot keep a house neat when at least one of three babies will be crying at any given point in time. And you cannot keep a house neat when you have wonderful friends and neighbors who come over just when the three babies are quiet, because it is much better to sit and tell stories about how sweet those babies are than it is to mop the bathroom. I learned that there was no shame in Aunt JJ folding my t-shirts at the table, because everybody wanted to do their part.

Kids don't remember a dusted mantle. Kids remember hearing *The Cat in the Hat* on the easy nights and the *Gilligan's Island* theme song when teeth are slowly growing in, or when recovering from an ileostomy.

Joy is contagious. In fact, our neighbor Maureen had so enjoyed feeding the babies and singing songs and reading stories that she decided to make her very own baby. She went to the bank and purchased herself some seed. You might think that this would be an easy process: Just go to the sperm bank and ask for a donor. But no, Maureen asked for the profiles of every single one of the donors for the four sperm banks she contacted. She read, filed, eliminated, cross-indexed, and finally came to our house for advice on a night when Uncle Jon and Uncle Tim were visiting.

Now, if Uncle Jon and Uncle Tim were experts on anything, it was picking out men. They're just not quite used to hanging on to them. We read the files of all the finalists and started sorting. It was kind of like one of those reality shows: "Who Wants to Be the Anonymous Daddy?"

Maureen said, "I want someone with a sense of humor, a strong chin, and good height."

Uncle Tim looked at the pile and said, "You do know that Brad Pitt is unlikely to have contributed to this sperm bank?" He picked up a half dozen forms and discarded them: "You don't want sperm from anybody from New Jersey. Trust me. I've tried it."

Papa eliminated all of the men with health problems and Uncle Jon eliminated all of the fashion victims. I eliminated all the people with spelling errors in their profiles, on the theory that if a guy is not bright enough to spell the word 'sperm' on a donor application, then you really don't want to have his children. By this time, a fair amount of forms had piled up on the floor. Miss Grrrl was happily chewing on a half-Japanese/half-Brazilian donor's papers. Vivienne, in Uncle Jon's arms, drooled on an application from an identical twin in Kansas.

We had gotten it down to four finalists when Tim spoke up and said, "Listen, Maureen, this is a crapshoot any way that you look at it. You really don't know anything more about these guys than if you went down to Pier 39, got a sailor drunk and had your way with him — a method, I might mention, that would be a lot cheaper than what you are doing now."

Armed with that advice, Maureen went home, took the top ten applications, shuffled them up, and picked the one off the bottom. She called the sperm bank and ordered a fresh dose. This was on a Monday. It takes some women as many as thirty injections to conceive; she was pregnant by Friday. Not only is joy contagious, but child creation as well.

So we were *not* sitting on the dock of the bay, *not* watching the fireworks on the pier, and *not* trying out the newest smart restaurant. We were staying at home, sitting in the rocker, feeding and burping and rocking the triplets, occasionally taking the dogs for a walk. Uncle Tim had often proclaimed that "the universe provides." I always retorted, "Provides what? Drama? Tragedy? A sitcom?" and he always gave me that Cheshire Cat smile in response.

But I knew, with Vivienne drooling over my t-shirt, that what had already been provided was enough.

CHAPTER 6

A Normal Week

September 8, 2003

"NORMAL" had taken on a whole new meaning. Before the triplets, *normal* meant that the house was clean, the dogs were brushed, and Brian/Papa and I had time to enjoy *Charmed* or *Star Trek* over a box of wine. Post baby arrival, *normal* meant that none of the infants had manifested any new developmental challenges while the house remained a mess, the dogs weren't brushed, and Papa and I had five minutes without babies crying to toss two bowls of Progresso Chicken Tuscany soup in the microwave and gulp them down before going back to the Terrific Trio.

Kyle and Vivian joined Joshua in the loud and painful process of teething, which meant that not only did they wail, but they sucked on whatever wasn't nailed down. Between the triplets and the Pekes, there was not an

75

unbitten piece of furniture in the blue bungalow.

Vivienne continued to grow. She outgrew her preemie clothes, her newborn clothes, her first quarter clothes, her zero-to-six month clothes, and was bursting out of her six-to-nine month clothes. At first I thought that she would be a world leader, but I began to suspect that she might be the first female professional linebacker. Not only was she growing rapidly, she could throw as well. Wolfcub learned that she had deadly aim with a binky.

We drove across the bridge for the six-month checkup. Amazing — we had kept them alive for half a year! Doctor Halberg smiled as she reviewed the charts, then insisted, "Vivienne and Joshua should start eating solid foods."

We drove home, stopping for Gerber's along the way, and began the next adventure. Joshua got the hang of pureed carrots right away, gulping down huge spoonfuls at a time. Kyle looked amused, but interested.

But in Vivienne's short six months, we'd erred. We had shown her *Barney* and *Little Einstein* but we never showed her *Dinner at Eight* or *My Dinner with Andre*. We must have inadvertently left her in front of the television when a John Belushi movie was on, convincing her that food is not something that necessarily belongs in the mouth, but makes an excellent projectile weapon. While Joshua ate an entire bowl of rice cereal, Vivienne decorated the baby chair, her clothes, her face, her hair, my face, my hair, and my t-shirt, as well as the dining room table. There was even a little bit of rice cereal hanging from Papa's chandelier.

Yes, the blue bungalow has one little bit of Lace Curtain Irish: a chandelier. Five years earlier, when Brian was touring extensively, I worked a lot of overtime and surprised him with Waterford crystal. What I did not know was that it would be shipped in pieces, so the day before Brian got back, Jon, Tim and I assembled a 223-piece chandelier, even jury rigging it to the ceiling. It was a monument to our butchness, more or less.

But our new life afforded no such leisure activities. Just walking in the door took an hour. First, alerted by the turn of the lock, Miss Grrrrl ran to the door, demanding to be scratched. Vivienne, seeing that I was paying attention to a Pekingese and not her, yowled and threw her binky. I then picked her up and as she cooed. Joshua, sensing that I opted to pay attention to the fair sex first, bellowed. Always the responsible father, I then placed Vivienne in the swing and picked up Joshua. This lasted about twenty seconds before Wolfcub waddled out of the bedroom, thinking that all of the noise meant food. I bent over and petted him, only to hear the mewling of Kyle, who had the softest and most pathetic cry of them all. He sounded like Pagliacci in the last act. You just *had* to stop and give him the time of day.

But picking up Kyle meant checking his diaper, which meant finding that his diaper was full, which meant cleaning his bottom, then finding the Ilex, then finding the antiseptic, then diapering him up again, by which time Vivienne decided that she was hungry, and cried again. I fed Vivienne, changed Vivienne, diapered Vivienne and by then Joshua was ready to eat. I fed Joshua, I changed Joshua, and I diapered Joshua while Miss Grrrl and Wolfcub headed for the back door. If I didn't get to the back door in time, they would leave whatever it was that they were gonna do on the lawn in the laundry room, and after I finished cleaning that up it was time for Miss Grrrl's kidney-friendly rice and chicken, which just about got me to the time for Kyle's bottle. And after the triplets settled down, we gave Miss Grrrl her subcutaneous fluids. It was Papa's job to inject the needle, and my job to lie down on the floor with her to calm her down. One of my advanced skills is remaining motionless to induce calm in others.

This new normal meant a new me. I saw the kids change every day, but it took someone else to see the change in me. One day, I was heating formula in a bit of a rush, because I knew that two-thirds of the triplets were nearing the end of their naps. I hit the faucet on the sink, and something broke. Don't ask me how or why; I'm not a plumber. But water gushed out. The dogs ran out to see just as the water spilled over the sink, the babies cried, and there I was, three o'clock in the afternoon, still in my red plaid bathrobe with the linoleum and the dogs drenched.

I called the first plumber I could find in the Yellow Pages, and this guy arrived in forty-five minutes. Nice, young, blue plumber shirt. He looked at the sink and said, "Looks like your lucky day."

"Huh?"

"Looks like your lucky day. You got a seven hundred and twenty-six dollar plumbing problem."

"Not feeling the luck," I sighed.

"No, look. See? The faucet broke."

"The faucet part I get. The luck part?"

"The luck part," he said as he turned the water off to the sink, "is that you got seven hundred dollars' worth of labor, twenty-six dollars' worth of parts. But you happen to know the plumber, even if you don't remember me." Somehow when the water turned off, the dogs stopped barking. "Five years ago, you were this tough old sergeant working midnights. There was a tweaker wandering around the dorm, demanding that you put the phone on so he could call his wife and tell her he was sorry. And you told this guy that he didn't need to call his wife at three in the morning. He needed to write her a letter, and tell her he was gonna give up this whole life."

Then I recognized him, now twenty pounds heavier, and thirty pounds happier. "And you did?"

"Yup. Clean for five years. Got a three-year old daughter. All of us in that jail used to joke about you. The mean old sergeant who talked straight. Only none of us thought you had a sweet side. Until today. So now you get your broken faucet fixed for the price of parts: twenty-six dollars. Welcome to fatherhood."

BY SHEER force of will, Kyle learned how to turn over. Turning oneself over is a major step in human development, halfway to doing calculus in your head. This meant that all three of them had hurdled another milestone. With all the flipping, the bungalow looked like the International House of Pancakes, what with each of the kids lying on their backs, rolling to their side, then falling to their stomach, then crying because they were no longer on their backs. Vivienne had more mass about her than the other two, and so she couldn't roll quite so easily. But there were ominous warnings from the three of them, signaling that they could all get from one side of their bodies to the other. They could also all press up on their arms, meaning that in a few weeks, they would master that next dreaded developmental milestone: crawling. Once the three babies began to crawl, all hope for sleep would be lost.

Over the previous few months, we had met with eleven social workers to discuss the foster-parenting-to-adoption trajectory. When we first took the triplets into our home, Meredith, the first of the social workers had told us, "The birth mother is a schizophrenic drug addict and the birth grandmother refuses to be tested for anything. The birth mother walked out on them in the hospital. The court removed their older brother from her care when the birth mother abused him. It is very unlikely that either one of them will ever be granted custody of the kids."

The court did offer reunification services to the family, but there were conditions placed upon them: Cici, the birth mother, would have to get clean and participate in a full psychological screening, and the birth grandmother needed to move the other four people out of her studio apartment. Ten of the eleven social workers told us that the babies would not be able to thrive with either the mother or the grandmother. On the most recent visit from Cici, the social worker observed that she tried to shove a chocolate bar in Kyle's mouth. The social worker present later told us, "No court would ever trust her with these children."

The eleventh social worker, however, had a different opinion. She was young, in her early twenties, and absurdly thin; Papa charitably referred to her as the "twelve-year-old anorexic twerp." On her first trip to visit us, she allowed that this was her first case.

"Where do you see the case going?" Papa asked, holding Joshua in his arms.

"I'm going to ensure reunification."

"What!?" Papa blurted.

"Surely you know that the kids would be more loved with the birth mother."

I jumped in. "Have you read the notes on this case?"

"Oh, yes, but I think they are exaggerating the schizophrenia. Who would have had sex with her if she was that crazy? Besides, the love of two men can never replace the love of a woman. A woman knows that kind of thing."

Although she surely meant well, I worried that her zeal to re-establish the bond of birth family blinded her to the conditions under which the children would live. We had seen the birth mother with the children; when we told her the doctor said they couldn't drink grape juice, she fed them grape soda instead.

We called Meredith. "This is bad," she said. "The new social worker has not gotten a sense of what's going on. But she's in control right now. If I were you I would hire a lawyer." She gave us the number of Ned Summerfield, a specialist who worked in Oakland. We called and made an appointment.

He reviewed all the reports as well as our notes and said, "There is no way that woman should be caring for these children. I'll take the case. But remember that the courts call the shots now, and the courts believe everything a social worker says."

There was a hearing set for September 30. At that hearing, the judge would decide whether to continue reunification services (which meant that the mother wasn't ready to raise the children, but that the court would give her whatever she needed to get there), halt reunification services (which meant that the court had decided that the mother would never achieve a minimal parenting threshold), or reunify the kids with the birth mother. The court would probably continue with present circumstances, which meant that Papa and I would remain the foster parents, and that the Twelve-Year-Old Anorexic Twerp would continue to pursue reunification with the birth mother. If she could prove in the next six months that the birth mother could provide a *minimal* level of care, then she would petition the court to move the triplets in with her. She took action, deciding to have visits with the kids at the birth grandmother's apartment to prove what a good mother she could be. Maybe she didn't realize that these kids deserved a little more than "minimal." Not to mention her overt discrimination against a gay couple.

Fostering is a hard term. When I was growing up, most of the parishioners in Saint Anthony of Padua parish sat on the right side, because that was the side of the Blessed Virgin. But I insisted on the left side because I always had sympathy for Saint Joseph. I called him the "frosted father of Jesus," and even then I knew that fostering meant doing all the work while knowing that a child was someone else's. But somewhere along the line, we came to know that these children were ours, not genetically, but in our hearts.

We weren't giving up. We had prayer circles in Pennsylvania, novenas in New Jersey, Wiccan blessings in the Lower Haight, candles lit in Colorado, meditations in Manhattan, kneeling in Johnstown, and masses in Saint Petersburg. And my brother Earl laying odds on Long Island. We were covered by the Catholics, the Christians, the Jews, the pagans, the Goddess Worshippers, the positive thinking agnostics, and the neo-Baptists. If angels existed, then Nurse Vivian and Diva were surely pulling for the triplets.

But it was easier to believe in Murphy's Law than miracles. During my forty-something years on the planet, I had honed cynicism into an art. Whenever a friend had counseled me to ask God, I smiled, sometimes even nodded my head, but most of the time, I'd thought that the chances of a deity going out of his or her way to help me were pretty slim. Whenever I looked for burning bushes, divided seas, or healed lepers, I was always disappointed.

But in my middle years, I realized that the universe was a pretty busy place, and you couldn't just go asking for transubstantiation on a daily basis. Some days, you just had to be happy with the small stuff.

ALBERT EINSTEIN once said that either you believe that
nothing is a miracle, or that everything is a miracle. Here
was our small miracle: The Twelve-Year-Old Anorexic
Twerp rang our doorbell one day and said, "I'm leaving
Alameda County. In fact, I'm leaving social work. I found
a much better paying job. You people don't seem to want
my help anyway."

Of course, the drama was not over; we had not yet
won. She had already made her report to the court and she
had already made her argument for reunification. She had
been fighting for it, and hoping it would be a feather in the
cap of her mercifully short social worker career.

Our lawyer called her a few hours later. She called me
back: "How dare you interrupt the process of reunification? I thought I told you what your place was."

Kyle cried softly in the background. I replied, "We are
not interrupting the process, and in fact we have cooperated
with the birth mother, despite the fact that she shakes the
children whenever they don't do what she wants. We have
cooperated with the birth grandmother, even when she
asked me how much money she could get every month
if she took the triplets in. We cooperated with all eleven
social workers that we had met since we first got the kids
six months ago. Simply put, we think the children will be
safer with us."

She replied venomously. "Just you wait until I brief

the county lawyer. She'll fight whatever you do. And I'm going to make sure that Samuel, your new social worker, takes care of the two of you."

Papa and I went to court one sleepless night later. Uncle Jon came with us for moral support. My nervousness is usually expressed by my small bladder and the need for chocolate. So Uncle Jon walked me to the men's room about twelve times and fed me Snicker's bars, cookies and whatever other chocolate he could find in the vending machines. Papa hung in there. I know how much he wanted a cigarette, wanted to chuck all those healthy habits we had gotten into for the sake of the children, but instead he sat, and tried to read a Mercedes Lackey novel.

The lawyer for that woman, the blue-suited Ms. Wong, approached our lawyer and yelled at him, "I'm going to do whatever I need to do to keep you out of the courtroom. And remember, the county is paying me. You're paying him (she pointed her manicured finger at Ned) by the hour. We can outlast you."

Four hours later, they called the case. The Alameda County Bailiff admitted us into a small chamber, with a judge's bench and three rows of seats. The judge asked, "Can the attorneys representing the case please introduce yourselves?"

The first lawyer stated that he represented the birth mother. (He had never seen the triplets.) The second lawyer said that he represented the triplets. (He had never seen the triplets.)

Ms. Wong said, "I am Ms. Wong and I represent the county."

Seeing our lawyer, the judge asked, "And you represent?"

Before Ned could stand up, Ms. Wong stood up, "Your honor, I motion that these three (pointing that manicured finger once again) be escorted out of the courtroom. Allow me to cite the Welfare and Institutions Code, which specifically prohibits..."

"Thank you," the judge commented, "Actually, I am quite familiar with the W and I code, as I am a justice of the family court. The code prohibits uninvolved parties, but it also states that anyone with a compelling interest in the children are welcome in the court." This time he looked directly at Papa and me. "I assume that you have a compelling interest?"

"Your honor," I stood up. "Yes, we are the foster parents, and even though we don't have any legal status, we are the ones who have been taking care of them all this time."

"I didn't know there were any issues," the judge commented.

"Well, sir, they were born prematurely, and they are hypertonic with developmental delays. In addition, we took care of the youngest boy's colostomy bag."

Ned Summerfield offered, "Your honor, these two are the only parents that the triplets have ever known. They have been caring for the babies since the day they left the hospital. If it please the court, we would like to file for *de facto* parent status, so that they can offer the testimony of the only people here who see the children on a daily basis."

The judge replied, "I cannot grant *de facto* status without a written request, but you may stay in my courtroom. If you have come this far, and waited all this time, you should at least know what is going on."

Ms. Wong stood up again, "Your honor, this case entails a discussion of confidential information about the birth mother, information which these two are *not* entitled to."

Ned rejoined, "Your honor, we care only about the children."

The judge looked at the paperwork in front of him and said to Ms. Wong: "Make your case about the birth mother's status and then these gentleman can return to the court."

We walked out for another wait. Ten minutes later a bailiff asked us into the courtroom. The judge ruled, "We will extend reunification services for six more months. But the children remain with Mr. Fisher and Mr. Paulson. After reviewing the notes, the court recognizes the extraordinary efforts that the two of you have made in raising these children."

This was good news and bad news. The birth mother still had the opportunity to reunite with the kids. The fair and honest side of me said that if Cici could really and truly get her act together — stay off of drugs, stay out of jail, take her psychotropic medicines, and cooperate with the medical staff — I could see her having the opportunity to raise the children, or at least partner with us in raising the children. Those were a lot of major stipulations, however, and I hadn't seen evidence of any of them being met yet.

Papa was the optimistic one of the two of us; I was the one who resisted miracles even when they slapped me in the face. So, this day's miracle, per Albert Einstein, was that we got to spend the next six months with the most beautiful triplets in the world. That day's lucky coincidence was that, for the first time ever, Kyle ate solid food. Six months ago, the doctors said he would be fed Pregestamil for years.

CHAPTER 7

Angel with a Busted Wing

October 7, 2003

NURSE VIVIAN and Pop got married on the rainiest day of November in 1947. She couldn't afford a wedding dress, and so she borrowed Aunt Rita's, who always blamed her for the stain on the sleeve afterwards. The night of the wedding, they drove to Niagara Falls for the honeymoon, with a side trip to relatives in Johnstown, Pennsylvania. Nurse Vivian got "in the family way" on the trip and delivered Earl nine months and eleven days after the wedding. Her mother-in-law, Sadie Toal, counted each of those last eleven days quite loudly to make sure that the rest of Glendale knew that her grandchild Harold Earl was legitimate.

Harold Earl (my brother) lived in the same house as Harold Aloysius (my father), Harold Edward (my cousin) and Harold Christian (my uncle) so to simplify matters, from then on he was called Earl.

Two years later, Nurse Vivian and Pop had a second son, whom they named Donald James Aloysius (making my middle name of Thaddeus less extraordinary). Thaddeus was at least the patron saint of the impossible; Aloysius patroned something like vestal virgins or tomato soup. Grandma Sadie loved Earl, and thought that the sun and moon rose and set over him. She thought Donald was the devil incarnate.

With two children in the house, Nurse Vivian and Pop decided that the honeymoon would have to be their last vacation for a while. Years went by and they worked and worked, saving up for the down payment for the house in South Ozone Park.

Finally, when the two boys were old enough to go to school, Nurse Vivian and Pop took a weekend away, leaving the kids with Grandma Sadie. They went to a resort in the Catskills. On the last day of the weekend, Pop got a phone call from Grandma saying that she wasn't quite sure how he did it, but little Donald had fallen off a roof and managed to break his collarbone. Nurse Vivian, being Irish Catholic and all, felt that the broken collarbone was her fault, and told Pop that they were never going away on vacation alone again. For the next six years, they took Earl and Donald to Camp Seneda, Boy Scout Camp and other family vacations. By the time I was born in the late 50s. Nurse Vivian and Pop had pretty much given up vacations as a lifestyle.

My mother was practical. When she found out that Earl had asthma, she made him take saxophone lessons to strengthen his lungs. Since Donald had a broken collarbone, she made him take accordion lessons to strengthen his back muscles. To this day, my brother's ability to generate polka music can be attributed to early childhood clumsiness. I regret that I never broke anything in my adolescence, or I might have developed a musical talent.

Last Sunday was the first full day that Papa and I had off from the triplets in months. Papa danced with ODC at Francis Ford Coppola's estate (the Niebaum Coppola Estate) in wine country. This was an annual event and I had dragged my stage-wife butt to it for years. One year I was seated at a table with a nice middle-aged man with a beard named George. We talked about all sorts of things before he asked me what I did for a living. I told him that I was a deputy sheriff, which he found to be fascinating. I asked him what he did for a living, and he told me that he was in film.

"Have you acted in any films that I might have seen?"

"Oh, I don't act."

"Well, then, have you worked on any films that I might have seen?"

"Well, I did make a few films that you might know."

I looked back blankly.

Everyone else at the table shouted, "*Star Wars!*"

George Lucas and I had a nice talk, and I told him that my nephew loves the *Star Wars* films and I had seen the trilogy twenty-four times, giving me something to gloat about with my nephew.

But this year, alas, I sat next to no celebrities. Instead, I sipped chardonnay in Napa Valley, watching the love of my life *plié* and *jeté* and *bourré* on stage.

After the show, as Papa was sucking down a bottle of Niebaum Coppola champagne, his phone rang.

"Hello, Brian? It's Jon."

"Yes?"

"I think that there's been an accident."

"With who?"

"Vivienne."

I got to the car in ten seconds and we were on the highway in twelve. We made it from the wine country to Children's Hospital in forty-one minutes. There were scorch marks on the side of the Vue.

Uncle Jon explained in the hospital, "She had been sitting with me and just as I was standing up, she pushed her arm at me. I just heard this tiny little sound." Jon felt terrible; we felt terrible. Vivienne certainly felt terrible. Doctor Halberg had the arm x-rayed and she explained, "This is a green stick break, a minor break in her arm.

We're going to put a tiny cast on it, and it will all be okay in a few weeks."

I called and left a message for Samuel, the newly-assigned social worker who had not met us yet. He showed up the next morning. He was a little older than me, thin gray hair receding fast. Faded blue eyes like chalkdust. He wore a silver cross on his chest, and he exuded that sexual ambiguity of born-again Christians. "Well, I suppose I had to come see this," he said.

The Twelve-Year-Old Anorexic Twerp had taught me that social workers do not always want justice; they want what they want. Of course, Samuel did what social workers do: filled out reports and offered tepid support, along the lines of, "Oh, please don't worry. I have seen foster parents create far worse injuries." I called Cici, who couldn't seem to wrap her thoughts around the concept. The birth grandmother got on the phone: "Who is paying for the doctor? Will she get more assistance money after this?"

Not knowing that answer, I handed the telephone to Samuel, who said, "Please don't worry. I wouldn't let anything happen to *your* children."

But the most important thing is that Vivienne would heal. Uncle Jon felt worse than she did.

I went looking into violin lessons for infants, figuring that Nurse Vivian would have made the best of this.

October 14, 2003

Nurse Vivian made three dishes well: Pea Soup, Beef Stew, and Spaghetti and Meatballs. Everything else was too exotic for her. She boiled all vegetables until they were good-and-cooked. She was the kind of woman who planned her meals around the leftovers they would yield. If you had Corned Beef and cabbage on Sunday, on Monday you would have leftover Corned Beef and boiled peas, and on Tuesday, you would have Corned Beef hash and boiled carrots. Dinner was served, invariably, at five-thirty every night. My brothers Earl and Donald figured out that it was best to eat big portions on Sunday because whatever wasn't eaten then would be re-heated the next day, and the day after, and the day after. We all dreaded Saturday night dinner.

We lived in South Ozone Park, about halfway between Aqueduct Raceway and Belt Parkway. Aqueduct Raceway was not high-class like Belmont. It was a lower-middle-class horse race track for guys who earned their paycheck every Friday and bet them away every Saturday. At just about five o'clock, all the guys who had lost big would come roaring out down Rockaway Boulevard and, racing towards Belt Parkway, hang a right turn on 130th Street where there was a dilapidated stop sign, pole bent and eclipsed by a large bush. Every Saturday night somebody would blow through the sign, hit another car, or crash into the light pole.

Because Nurse Vivian was the only nurse for about five blocks in the old Irish neighborhood, one of the kids would come banging on the aluminum door, crying, "Nurse Vivian! Somebody hurt their nose/tooth/arm..." The ambulance from Mary Immaculate Hospital had a notoriously slow driver who liked to slip out for a drink or two on Saturday afternoon before making any pickups, so my mother would run out the door with a sewing needle and some old handkerchiefs, and figure out how to splint the broken nose/tooth/arm. When in doubt, she applied pressure and elevated. Donald and Earl would run out after her, not wanting to miss any blood and gore.

I ate very slowly on Saturday nights, knowing that the first big loser to crash on 131st Street would empty out the house, giving me the chance to evenly distribute my hash and boiled carrots on my absent brothers' plates. If there were too many carrots, I hid some under the painter's cloth in the living room.

This all came to a stop in 1965, when Nurse Vivian led all the other mothers to drive their baby carriages into the intersection of Sutter Avenue and 131st Street. They parked there, even got their picture in the Long Island Press, and kept up the pressure until Queens County agreed to put up a new stop sign.

Joshua, Vivienne, and Kyle had been living with us for six and a half months by then, and Miss Grrrl and Wolfcub felt shorted on attention. Before the triplets, we used to walk them four or five times a day, brush them out every other day, and bathe them every week. Miss Grrrl had not had a bath since the day the duplets moved onto Winding Way. But Miss Grrrl didn't resent the attention that the kids got; instead she lay under their crib and growled at anyone she didn't trust getting near her brood. But, as an eminently practical dog, she did run out after me every time that I went into the kitchen for a bottle of formula, confident that if the babies were getting something, she at least deserved a cookie or two.

We had been feeding the triplets formula with no color and less taste for six months. How did I know it doesn't have taste? Because I tried it. Haven't you always wondered? It tastes like milk wrapped in plastic. Not as bad as Nurse Vivian's Saturday night dinner, but… needless to say, after six months of it, the kids were ready to try out some real food. As I mentioned, Doctor Halberg had agreed that the duplets should be initiated to solid foods: "Start with squash and carrots. If you start with bananas you will never get to carrots."

After the John Belushi incident, Vivienne, true to form, gulped down the squash. She ate so many carrots that she started saying, "What's up, Doc?" Kyle, ever the dainty one, was willing to take a sip, and then another sip, but, really, he just wanted to savor the experience of solid foods. But the big surprise was Joshua. Joshua was eating two bowls of cereal to each one consumed by Kyle. Joshua ate enough squash to start his own club. Because of his enthusiasm, I naturally assumed that carrots would be a wonderful adventure for him. I got out the high chair and made a big fuss about setting him up with his favorite bib. He cooed. He smiled. He batted at the table. I thought that all would go well. He took his first taste of carrot and with those big brown eyes of his, he looked up at me and drooled carrot all the way down his bib. Just then, the bottle warmer beeped, causing Miss Grrrrl to bark. In the one second I took to turn away, Joshua picked up his bowl of mashed carrots and threw it across the room. Miss Grrrrl, the kitchen counter, the kitchen floor, and my white t-shirt were all covered in carrot mash.

At least Miss Grrrrl got a bath out of it.

CHAPTER 8

The Feast of All Souls

November 3, 2003

T HERE were days when I was lucky to brush my teeth. Sometimes, it got to three in the afternoon, and I was still in my bathrobe. But then there were those special days when it was all easy.

I took the triplets to the doctor on such a day. The nurses cooed. The social workers smiled (except for Samuel, of course, who seemed unamused by infants).

Kyle weighed thirteen pounds, three ounces; Joshua weighed seventeen pounds, one ounce; Vivienne weighed seventeen pounds, five ounces. Kyle was twenty-three-and–a-half inches tall, Joshua was twenty-four-and-a-half inches tall, and Vivienne was twenty-five-and-a-half inches tall. If you put them all together, you'd get a six–foot-two long, forty-seven-pound baby.

They were beginning to hit the developmental

markers that they were supposed to hit (since they were two months premature, you had to think of them as five-and-a-half-month old kids rather than seven-and-a half-month-old kids). So, they were actually doing things on schedule now. Joshua grabbed at everything, including Papa's chest hair. Lacking such, I suffered less. Vivienne, who was just waiting for the right motivation, would soon sit up without our help. Kyle had already asked me for the keys to the car. (At least that's what it sounded like to me.)

During the holiday season, Brian danced with ODC, where he played the boy in *The Velveteen Rabbit* as well as at Berkeley Ballet, where he danced the role of little Fritz in *The Nutcracker*. He had been doing this for thirteen years now: thirteen years of playing little Fritz against Berkeley Ballet's Clara, always played by their best student of the year. We had seen a generation of little girls progress from angel to gumdrop to sheep to *corps de ballet* and finally, to Clara. A good number of them are already retired from dance and were on their second career. At 41, Brian was feeling the pressure, kind of like Margot Channing in *All About Eve*. But he still out-danced all the other dancers, and could *jeté* and *plié* and arabesque with the best of them.

ON FRIDAY, we dressed up the triplets as matching pumpkins. Oh, I imagined that later in life they could pick zombies or vampires or whatever, but we drove them to the pumpkin patch, and they were all about the size of pumpkins themselves, so instead of the Great Pumpkin, Charlie Brown, we had the triplet pumpkins.

Friday night was Halloween night, or Samhain (pronounced *Sow-en*; don't ask), and we celebrated the night in a traditional way. Uncle Tim, a practicing Wiccan, had established a gay male coven in San Francisco a few years earlier and was determined to do the holiday right.

"Your own coven, Tim?" I challenged.

"I'm taking after you."

"Tim, I am many things, but a practicing witch is not one of them."

"No, but you see, a coven is a family. A created family. That's what you do. You collect people and shape them into a family. You took in the orphans. You took me in. And the down-on-their-luck dancers, and the wrestler, and the kittens and stray puppies."

"You mean I run a hotel for lost souls."

"Lost angels, more like it. Come to our Samhain festival."

"You know, you fancy yourself the Endora of this coven, but you're really the Aunt Clara."

I prided myself on keeping an open mind about all things. So I thought that if I could go to a Catholic Church on Sunday despite my reservations about the Pope, then I could go to a Pagan ritual "when the veil between the worlds is at its thinnest."

It turned out that the people who attended Catholic Church were cut from the same cloth as those who attended Pagan rituals. They were all steeped in ritual, and like the genuflecting Catholics I had seen the Sunday before, the pagans were determined to make the pentagram in the exact right way. Samhain, a "Holy Day of Obligation," is the joining of the community to celebrate a common theme. The etymological root of the word "liturgy" comes from "a service to man." A good liturgy therefore should bring a community together, tell a story that can serve as a lesson, and celebrate the community by sharing bread, food, song, and dance. A good liturgy should leave you with hope.

If anyone was good at servicing men, it was Uncle Tim.

This ritual was conducted in a de-sanctified chapel and began with a silent procession and anointing. Okay, you want Only-in-San Francisco Cool? It was the same building as the sanitarium scene in *Vertigo*.

We walked through catacombs (well, technically storage basements, but it felt like catacombs) by candlelight and came to a table covered with memorabilia, mainly in pictures, of those we loved. We each took a moment to remember those who had passed and to talk about what we had learned from them. I touched the photo of Nurse Vivian, the sepia tone print of a smiling woman in a starched white uniform with nurse's cap. Next to it I had placed a picture of Diva, lying on the couch, peacefully chewing on a potato. Tim touched a photo of Tony, his lover, in his chef's outfit, holding a whisk, trying to look all Iron Chef. Tony was perhaps the most intolerable of all of Tim's lovers, and Tim spent close to five years figuring out how to leave him. But Tony in death has become a saint. Death burns off all of the petty quarrels, bickering, and nonsense, and leaves us only with love and joy.

After speaking about our loved ones, we walked through a shadowed passageway to a doorway where water was sprinkled on our faces and the Wiccans encouraged us to shout, "They are dead, but I am alive!" We then stepped into bright light where people were dancing and singing, honoring the dead by celebrating the life in front of us. When the dancing stopped, we sat in a circle and told stories. Tim handed me a book and from it I read to everyone an invocation of the Goddess, addressing her many names including Astarte, Ceridwhen, and Isis. I got to thinking that they might as well have thrown in Mary the Virgin Mother, because, after all, Samhain is a celebration of the energy to create, to grow, to nurture and to manifest the divine.

This past year, the theme for me had been about learning to embrace the nurturing, kinder side of my soul, less of the jailhouse keeper. The triplets were an outer manifestation of that gift.

Tim, resplendent in a flowing black velvet robe, winked and whispered to me, "The invocation, a blessing of all new life, is always read by someone who has brought life into the world in the past year." Tim had invited me to the ceremony because of the triplets. Hard to see myself as the Earth Mother, but there you go.

After the reading, we each drew a Tarot card for the year. I pulled the High Priestess, a symbol of learning to embrace the nurturing and intuitive side of the self. We then shared cake and wine.

I have no idea what kind of god there is out there. I only know that I had met in the past year a hundred people who have shown me that it does not matter whether you believe in virgin births or Tarot cards. It matters only how your faith brings you to make yourself, and this world, a little bit better.

That Sunday, Uncle Tim volunteered to watch the triplets while Papa and I went to church. We dropped them off in his little studio and promised to return in an hour. At mass, they finally sang a hymn I knew (*All Creatures of our God and King....*). Papa prefers when they don't play hymns that I know because I sing a little too robustly. I was thinking of joining the choir.

The priest gave one of the best sermons I have ever heard in my life. I had gone to church for the first twenty-one years of my life but I had slept through more than a thousand sermons. I came from the kind of family that measures a successful mass by its length. My brothers both loved Father Fusco at Saint Anthony of Padua, who was famous for his thirteen-minute mass.

Long story short: I walked away from the church at twenty-one, mad at the Pope and all his crazy rantings against women and gay men. Years passed, and I'd recently wandered back into the Church. Brian and I agreed when we started filling out fost-adopt paperwork that we wanted our children to have a focus for values. Not that children cannot learn them in other ways, but for me the Catholic Church was a foundation. Even when I walked away, there was a yearning inside me, an emptiness. I realized that the Feast of the Epiphany those years ago truly was an Epiphany for me. That parish had taught me how much I wanted to belong to the family of mankind, and what kind of father I wanted to be.

Now that we were church-going, I had been trying to pay attention more than in my youth, but found that years of training taught me that the sermon is merely a pretext for a twenty-minute catnap.

But this time Father Phelan quoted Oscar Wilde: "Every saint has a history, and every sinner has a future."

That's what it's all about, isn't it? Doesn't matter whether we meet in a Mosque or a Temple or Stonehenge, we gather together in community because we believe in change; we believe in what each of us can become. Redemption may not pay off in an eternity with a cloud and a harp, but in the satisfaction that I created beauty and honor in my little corner of the universe, in the blue bungalow.

After church, we returned to Uncle Tim's studio, where he had the three little angels lined up on his bed, and he was taking pictures. We all drove home to the bungalow, and as a way to continue our weekend of honoring the dead, I dug a big hole in the backyard for Diva's ashes. We invited the family over and as we spread her ashes in the ground, Uncle Tim prayed a Wiccan blessing and Lori added a touch of the Catholic by throwing a spade of dirt. We planted a fig tree on top of her ashes and told stories about Diva, the world's best sleeper, the only dog who enjoyed potatoes. Not the brightest dog in the world, but certainly the sweetest.

As brunch is the ritual meal of gay men, we ate bagels, eggs, and sausage. (Uncle Tim ate tofu sausage, which was just as bad as it sounds). We drank mimosas (Uncle Tim drank Virgin Mimosas), and Uncle Jon commented, "Closest he's been to a virgin in twenty years." This was the joke that Uncle Jon told every time that Uncle Tim drank a Mimosa. The triplets ate strained bananas, which we felt they'd earned for the day. Miss Grrrl and Wolfcub ate real sausage, and declined the potatoes.

We celebrated the cycle of life and the manner in which each generation contributes to the next generation, sometimes in ways that we cannot understand. We live in a circle, spiraling upward, and bringing joy into the lives of others is the most important thing we can do. And in that, I hoped I lived as well as Diva.

CHAPTER 9

Say Cheese!

November 24, 2003

EVERY THANKSGIVING, Nurse Vivian went all out and served a high-class meal. She used the good stainless steel, china, and real cloth napkins. She served hot *hors d'oeuvres* consisting of miniature frankfurters wrapped up in Pillsbury biscuits, as well as olives and celery in a clear glass dish. The next course was my personal delight: shrimp cocktail, the kind that you could buy in a six-pack from King Kullen Supermarket. The shrimp came in little glass jars with metal lids, meaning that we also got new juice glasses at this time of year. She saved the Welch's jelly jars that contained the pictures of the Flintstones for the same purpose.

Nurse Vivian was in many ways a smart woman, the first woman in our family to finish high school, let alone go to nursing school. And she was a superstitious Irish daughter from a coal town in Pennsylvania. So whenever there were two pieces of bad luck in a row (a ripped pair of pants following upon chicken pox, or perhaps a death in the family), Nurse Vivian would take one of those juice glasses and throw it against the stoop, saying that bad luck always comes in threes, so the third bad luck might as well be a lost juice glass.

I missed my mother's quirkiness, like the way she used to feed Captain Crunch cereal to the birds in the South Ozone Park winter. On some days I realized that Nurse Vivian's superstitions were all too often right, but I'd like to think that the opposite is true now, that our good luck, rather than our bad luck, now comes in threes, or triplets.

When Papa and I met eighteen years earlier, I worked in the china department at Macy's in downtown Newark, New Jersey. We didn't have much money then, but we allowed ourselves a luxury each month: a plate or soup bowl from Virtue, a china pattern with a silver border and white roses outlined in a soft blue. Eighteen years later, we had a home and a car and a second pair of sneakers, and the distance between paychecks was not as large as it used to be. Most importantly, we had a china service for eight. In our little blue bungalow on the edge of San Francisco, we seldom had use for this luxury, except on Thanksgiving Day.

We moved the ancient couch and television against

the wall, and the dining room table to the center of the room. A rickety slab of wood won in a divorce from a particularly evil ex-lover, the table could have become an antique in the hands of better caretakers. However, we had lost the screws that attached the legs, and allowed Miss Grrrrl and Diva and Wolfcub to teethe on them. On top of this table, we placed the cream and gold linen tablecloth that Amanda gave me when her mother died. Amanda insisted that her mother would have wanted this heirloom of her long Jewish heritage to grace the table of two outrageous goyim queens. There must be a stitch of Hebrew grace in the thread, for we have never spilled as much as a drop of gravy on the cloth. Papa washed each piece of Virtue, dried it, and set it one dish at a time, onto the table. We had a dishwasher by now, but he insisted on doing it by hand. His dining room table, like his dancing, would always be precise and beautiful.

Our crystal consisted of a hodgepodge of Crystal D'Arque and Superman Pepsi glasses, plus whatever wine glasses I hadn't broken in the previous year. Mine read "Souvenir of Mondavi Winery." From a bodega on Mission Street that stays open on Thanksgiving Day came yellow roses in an old Riunite bottle.

I didn't know if I even liked Thanksgiving. Like California, it struck me as too sunny. Most holidays were tough for queens like me. Oh sure, we had our Halloween, but even that had been co-opted by straight people from across the bridges who came down to the Castro because they couldn't entertain themselves. But the sit-down holidays intimidated me. I had always felt as though I was sneaking into these rituals about the birth, death and re-birth of a god, hoping that no one would notice that I didn't really belong. At the same time I didn't want to miss out on the fun.

But Thanksgiving could be great, once you got past all the weight gain and the football. What I liked was the sharing. Thanksgiving gave me a chance to decide who family was. My first family, which consisted of my Pop, Nurse Vivian, Brother Earl and Brother Donald, didn't go for the sentimental. We were five impossibly different people living under the flight path of Idlewild Airport in Ozone Park. But we belonged to each other during Thanksgiving, if only during halftime.

At nine o'clock in the morning every year, Donald and I sat down to watch the Macy's Parade. We lived less than fifteen miles away from Herald Square but instead of taking the elevated J train to the subway to the city to watch the live version, we always watched from our house while eating Captain Crunch and orange juice that we had frozen into a plastic cup the night before. Donald liked watching the marching bands while I sat on the floor, playing with my Ken Doll and waiting for the Rockettes.

By an arcane method that determined the pecking order of the sisters and the sisters-in-law for the remaining part of the year, we rotated between Aunt Rita's, Aunt Mildred's, and our home on holidays. The Aunt who got Christmas was the matriarch for the year; the aunt who got Thanksgiving ranked just below her; the aunt who got Easter was relegated to bottom feeder status. From the day in 1947 when my Mother threw up on the sleeve of Aunt Rita's wedding dress, the two never liked each other. But they both agreed not to invite my father's older brother, Uncle Charlie. He and his wife, Aunt Ann, never owned a television, so by the mid-sixties they had fifteen children, too many to invite to any of the other three houses at any time. Of the three homes, I preferred Aunt Rita's exotic orange aluminum home in Hicksville. Unlike our home, there was a huge couch in the living room.

While the ten cousins played Monopoly, Uncle Leon served cocktails at the bar in the finished basement. Pop drank bourbon and water and Nurse Vivian drank Presbyterians, a mix of Seagram 7 and ginger ale. Grand Aunt Bea always drank Scotch. Neat. During cocktails, Aunt Rita served the exotic *hors d'oeuvres*, like chestnuts wrapped in bacon and drowned in barbecue sauce. Or Cheese Whiz on Triscuits.

The Paulson moment of fame: Nurse Vivian had been a contestant on a New York television show, "Stairway to the Stars." She won a set of matching stainless steel silverware in a hard plastic carrying case. At every holiday she brought that carrying case and we placed the utensils around the gold-rimmed china that had been our Grandmother's pattern. One year, Aunt Rita borrowed Grand Aunt Bea's set of crystal, only to watch her second daughter, Janie, spill the tray of glasses down the basement stairs. After that, the kids drank from Welch's jars.

The adult table seated Uncle Leon and Aunt Rita in her brown velvet dress, Uncle Eddie and Aunt Mildred in a floral print too large for her ample bosom, and Pop and Nurse Vivian, in her red chiffon cocktail dress that I tried on only once. Somewhere past puberty, by another mysterious rite of passage that I did not understand, the cousins graduated to the adult table. First Robert, then Carol. By 1968, Mimi and I were alone at the bridge table in the kitchen.

The Toals ignored the influence of Vatican II, so grace began with the sign of the cross, invoking the Father, the Son (head bow) and the Holy Ghost. No hand holding like those Italians down the block. No spontaneous gratitude like the Protestant families on TV. Just the sonorous voice of Uncle Eddie: *"Bless us, Oh Lord, and these thy gifts, which we are about to receive, from thy bounty..."* A toast followed. Cousin Mimi and I with our cider longed for the day that we too could have Andre Cold Duck.

Our Shanty Irish low-classiness allowed us to skip healthy courses such as soup or salad. Leave that to the Lace-Curtain Irish who could afford fruit on the table, even when no one in the house was sick. Like I said, our one pretense was those King Kullen shrimps, awash in cocktail sauce, floating on a chunk of iceberg lettuce.

Then we went directly to the turkey. Olives and celery stalks rested in the relish tray uneaten. Aunt Rita stuffed her bird with chestnuts because Uncle Leon liked it that way. Nurse Vivian stuffed her bird with sausage because Pop liked it that way. Aunt Mildred made a bowl of each dressing because she hated arguments. The rest of the meal included mashed potatoes, turnips with bacon, canned peas and carrots, canned cranberry sauce (usually forgotten), and Nurse Vivian's secret recipe: string bean casserole (a bag of frozen green beans mixed with Campbell's Cream of Mushroom Soup and topped with Mrs. Paul's Onion Rings.)

After seconds and thirds were consumed, the men hustled their bountiful buttocks into the living room to watch football as the aunts washed dishes and discussed the Alice Crimmins case, hair colors, and which children had gotten left back in which grade. Cousin Mimi and I watched *The Miracle on 34th Street* on the black and white television in the basement (Aunt Rita had *two* television sets). The pies were served between games. Thick-crusted apple was the favorite, but just so that no one would go home hungry, the three aunts provided caramel pecan, pumpkin and lemon with thick peaks of meringue. I sat at the kitchen table through many a pie baking, and learned the secrets of mince meat and even rhubarb, but never once did I figure out the magic in that meringue. I asked Aunt Mildred what my mother's secret was and she smiled, "You've got to beat the meringue with the right spoon." But she never did say which spoon that was.

Nurse Vivian even percolated coffee, rather than boiling water for Instant Maxwell. Grand Aunt Bea finished off the desserts with Heavenly Hash, a mixture of canned fruit cocktail, walnuts and marshmallow Fluff. This left me just blurry enough to get sick from Pop's cigar on the drive home.

But this Thanksgiving, Nurse Vivian was gone. Pop flew out from Florida. In his late eighties with a heart condition and his eyesight going, he still wanted to meet "his grandchildren." The day before Thanksgiving, he helped me bake the pies for the feast for the homeless at Most Holy Redeemer. As we got in the car, Pop said, "Let's go to Ikea."

"Ikea? It's across the bridge."

"I've got to do something. For Nurse Vivian." We drove to the Ikea in Emeryville, and Pop walked over to the furniture section. "Pick out a kitchen table," he said.

"Pop, we didn't fly you out here to buy us a kitchen table."

"Listen, you remember the house on South Ozone Park? Remember the living room?"

"With the stepladder?"

"Yes. Your mother never worried about a couch, but she worked a bunch of overtime shifts to buy that kitchen table. Nurse Vivian would want you to raise those triplets around a kitchen table." And so, we picked out a table together, oval-shaped, easy to assemble, and that night, we set three high chairs around the table, and with Pop and Papa, we celebrated the eve of Thanksgiving. We said grace. We had meatloaf. The triplets had oatmeal and applesauce. Didn't even matter what we had the next day.

Growing up, my favorite day during the holiday season was the Friday after Thanksgiving. After breakfast, the one Friday morning of the year that the Pope allowed us to eat meat, Nurse Vivian, Pop, and I drove out to Great Eastern Mills Department Store where Pop and I spent hours picking out boxes of Christmas Cards. We got one box with a manger scene for religious friends, one box saying "Season's Greetings" for all of our nice Jewish friends who were Christian enough to participate in card exchange, two boxes with reindeer for families with children, two boxes of the postcard-sized cards for the acquaintances we felt obligated to send a card to, one box with gold foil envelopes for close friends we wanted to impress, and one box with sparkles for our relatives. Dad picked out only individual non-boxed card for Grand Aunt Bea: Santa Claus covered in brown yelling at a red-faced reindeer, "Rudolph, you idiot! I said the SCHMIDT house."

In the decades that followed, I have given up on New York and heterosexuality, but I insist on those Christmas Cards, if for no other reason than to make a list of my friends each year.

FOR EIGHTEEN holiday seasons, Papa and I had woken up the day after Thanksgiving, picked up coffee and dough-nuts at Ann's Schneider Bakery in New Jersey — or chai tea lattés at Starbucks in our San Francisco years — and then taken the one posed photograph of the year. This served as our Christmas card, and we sent it to everyone we considered family. To us that meant Amanda, who remembered me when I had a full head of hair, and Tim, the Wiccan who still loves Christmas. We wrote to the family of ex-lovers, including Papa's lumberjack, my Mafia hit man, Papa's Broadway producer, and my cowboy named Theodore.

We'd gotten funnier as the years passed, with less glamour and more dogs. There was the year we dressed them in tutus, doing the dance of the Sugarplum Peking-gese; and there was the year with all five of us in the manger scene, the angels on Mount Davidson ("Pekingese We Have Heard on High"); and who could forget all five of us with pointed hats and broomsticks for "Christmas Greetings from Dogwarts School of Witchcraft and Wizardry"? As the cards grew more elaborate, we drafted Jon, Tim and Lori to help.

One bright sunny November morning, Papa, Tim, Jon, Miss Grrrl, Diva, Wolfcub, and I all drove up to the top of Twin Peaks. The theme for this card was "Christmas Greetings from the Planet Krypton" and we had wrestled Miss Grrrl, Diva and Wolfcub into Superman costumes. Just as we started trudging up the hill, a busload of Japanese tourists got out and started snapping away.

"Is this American tradition?" they asked.

"Yes, I said, "this is very much an American tradition."

And as with every year, Jon started snapping pictures and Tim stood behind Jon, yelling at the dogs and holding up cheese to make them look toward the camera.

When Papa asked me about the Christmas card this year I felt funny. As I sat on the couch I thought about how things are tentative with Miss Grrrl, who has kidney failure, and Wolfcub, with the heart condition. Uncle Tim, who always stands behind Uncle Jon, now had a T-cell count of six and a viral load of 476,000. And we had these superb triplets, but we knew that forces in the county were working against us. Samuel had even said,

"I think they're ready for an overnight visit." God help us all.

Who knew if Kyle, Vivienne and Joshua would even be with us a year from now? Did I want to take a picture of a family that existed only in the moment and might be gone by the next year?

I looked down on the floor and watched Joshua. He looked up at me and smiled. I smiled back at him and he waved. I waved back and all at once, for the first time ever, he started crawling towards me. Kyle smiled and Vivienne laughed as if to say, "Hah!!! One of us is finally mobile. Just you wait and see what we do to the house now."

Joshua had gotten it before I did. Family was not a permanent thing that stands frozen in a photograph. Family was a living, growing, crawling entity. How we defined family yesterday may not be how we define family tomorrow. We had only today. We had only today for this family of these three babies, these dogs and these two fathers. And this moment in time was the wonder of crawling. Why not take a picture to remember this day as best we could?

Papa and I went shopping and a couple of hundred dollars later, he was finally satisfied that we had the right outfits for the three kids. We had our theme: the triplets dressed all in red velvet, like the final scene of "White Christmas," with Vivienne looking uncannily like

Rosemary Clooney. Papa and I wore Santa Claus outfits with those little tiny gold rimmed glasses. We decked the dogs out as elves. Aunt Lori, Uncle Jon and Uncle Tim came over to charm the kids into smiling and the dogs into looking at the cheese behind the camera. Humor, after all, had always been the thing that kept this family together. Of course, the dogs kept running out of the frame, I kept dropping the glasses and Joshua kept wiggling. When Vivienne and Kyle burst into tears, I kissed Papa and we had a byline: *I Saw Daddy Kissing Santa Claus.*

On Thursday, as we dished out the turkey and the string bean casserole and the garlic mashed potatoes, we were grateful for sweat pants, and grateful for knowing the joy of these babies, these dogs, these friends. The happiness of the past year was made so much greater through the reflection of the eyes of our family, our loved ones, our friends. My family and friends had given the gift of themselves in this past year, whether that was through babysitting, or bringing diapers over, or changing colostomy bags, or bringing us donuts in the hospital, or writing e-mails to wish us luck or praying that all of this worked out.

Sometimes we gays had to re-invent tradition. I realized that what I told that Japanese tourist was right. This *is* a tradition, one we had just invented. Tradition is the story we tell that announces that we belong together. And who knows who would be on the card next year? Who knows who would take the photo? But I did know who my family was right then. Crawling and all.

The next morning I joined the church choir. My faith was as wobbly as my bass voice, but as they lit the first candle of the Advent wreath, and as we sang, *Oh come, Oh come, Immanuel,* Vivienne cooed, and I knew it was the right thing.

CHAPTER 10

All I Want for Christmas
Is My Two Front Teeth

Christmas 2003

A FTER FOUR months, it finally happened. We woke up and started the old diaper and oatmeal routine, changing and feeding Kyle, then changing and feeding Joshua, then picking up Vivienne. Picking up Vivienne was one of the little miracles of life. The boys smiled at me, but they were marking time through the diaper changing until they could get to morning formula. But not Vivienne. She giggled the minute that I picked her up, as if to say that her scheme finally worked, and with those pesky boys out of the way, she could finally sit down with me, process the morning, and make plans for the day. I imagined that she would be a fierce coffee drinker later in life, but for now we had only instant oatmeal and Similac.

That morning, however, after four months of drooling

and sucking and crying and complaining, Vivienne looked up at me and giggled and there, resting comfortably on the top of her gum, was a proud new tooth. Once again the world changed. It was only nine months ago that she and brother Joshua moved into the house, and all they could do was sleep and eat and produce the end product of eating, but this week they were producing teeth and crawling.

We had baby-proofed the home a year earlier. Or so we thought. The triplets had discovered mobility, and their perspective on baby proofing was very different than an adult's perspective. Joshua was the most ambitious explorer of the three and in the past few weeks he had discovered that CD cases made excellent drums, and that Royal Kanin dog food was not only delicious but also quite easy to throw. The kitchen looked like a mortar field.

So when we got our Christmas tree, we thought that we would put it at baby-proof level.

We took our Christmas trees seriously. Every year, right after the Christmas cards, Brian marched me out to the Delancey Street Christmas tree yard. We went there because the proceeds go to support people with substance abuse issues and because they have the biggest selection on our side of the city. The first few years we went, I walked around the lot with Brian and made serious comments about each of the trees. But by then I knew better. My job was to remain quiet until Papa had examined every single tree on the lot and picked out the two bushiest and biggest ones there. He'd then hold them up in front of me and say, "Which do you like?" When I pointed out one, he'd say, "We'll get both."

At home, we hauled out nineteen cartons of Christmas ornaments. Papa and I were packrat decorators. We saved Christmas decorations from our earliest, and I mean *earliest*, days. For me, the first ornament dated back to the 1960s, when I made the manger scene out of clothespins and paint. Brian's was a green cardboard ornament cut out in the shape of a bell and covered with macaroni. These ornaments were like us, more than four decades old, and although age had not treated them kindly, memory did. There was even a sparkly cardboard ornament that my Grandmother had put on her Christmas tree in 1941.

The family story goes that she put the ornaments on the tree the first week of December. After the Pearl Harbor attack, FDR declared war on December 8th. Christmas came and went and Grandpa Carl asked her when she was taking down the tree. She looked him square in the eye and said, "Not till my son Harold comes back from the army and sees it." Harold did not get a leave until April of that year. But the tree was still up, looking a little worse for wear. She said that she would keep it up until my father took out Hitler. Each one of her twenty-five grandchildren got an ornament from that tree.

1989 was the worst year for our Christmas tree. I was working as a salesclerk for Lackluster Video and Brian had stopped dancing and was working part time in a library. We had barely enough money for the rent and had decided not to get a tree. But on Christmas Eve, the guy who was running this Jersey City Christmas tree lot broke down and handed me a Charlie Brown tree, saying, "Here, kid, it ain't like I'm gonna sell any of these tomorrow."

I dragged the bedraggled pine home and hauled it up all five stories to our apartment on Barrow Street. One neighbor stopped by with a bottle of wine, another one came with cookies, and before we knew it, we had a little impromptu party. We went to bed with visions of sugarplums dancing in our head.

At three in the morning, we woke to a loud crack. We ran to the living room and there was our tree, laden down with all those ornaments, tipping off its base and cracking the window five stories above Kennedy Boulevard. The remaining ornaments lay scattered on the floor, all except for one of the clothespin magi I had made. Miss Grrrl thought it made an excellent chew toy.

We refer to that year as the year our Christmas tree attempted suicide.

This year, of course, we had to get three trees: one for Kyle, one for Joshua, and one for Vivienne. We baby-proofed the trees by putting all three of them up on tables, but it only took Joshua an hour or two to figure out how to reach the bottom branches. I was kept busy rescuing unicorns, Barbies, and Batmen afterward. We actually had a Waterford ornament on our tree and about five hundred ornaments that Nana gave us over the years. A few years before, in the pre-triplet days, I hand-painted a bunch of ceramic ornaments for Papa to represent all of the major dance pieces he had ever done, including *The Velveteen Rabbit, La Cage Aux Folles, The Statue of Liberty, The Music Man,* and *The Wizard of Oz.* The only thing you could say for sure was that gay men had decorated the tree.

Christmas was community-oriented in the Irish neighborhood of South Ozone Park. As kids we went from house to house decorating the trees, and at each house, families offered the adults a Rheingold beer or two. By the fifth tree, the ornaments started to drift with the decorators and the garlands wouldn't be hanging as neatly as they did at the first house.

The year that Papa and I moved into the blue bungalow, we revived the ornament party. The bungalow was the perfect home for a Christmas party: fireplace, piano, big kitchen. Our friends and family came over and brought an ornament from their tree, and took an ornament from our tree, and in that way, our home was a part of their home and their home was a part of our home. Oddly enough, the best ornaments came from our non-Christian friends, mainly because our Jewish, Muslim, and Wiccan friends did not feel bound by all that nativity business and could focus instead on the decorative nature of light. Uncle Jon always showed up with a handcrafted ornament, whether that be stained glass or snipped tin. Uncle Tim's usually involved magical totems or naked Santas.

Some traditions ended that year. Tim didn't have a lot of Christmases left in him, and Miss Grrrl was nearing her expiration date as well. And of course, the status of the triplets remained in doubt. Yet even as I considered time passing, that Christmas was about finding a new me. We celebrated Christmas with our children, and even if they eventually were returned to the birth mother, I learned that I was always meant to parent children, in whatever form that took. The experience taught me how to relax about the future and sit with the present.

The day before Christmas Eve, we drove the triplets to the adoption agency so that the birth mother could have the overnight visit. She arrived forty-five minutes late, which Samuel excused by "all that holiday traffic."

We walked the triplets to her car, a red Chevrolet convertible. "Where are the car seats?" Papa asked.

"Oh, I don't have any," she explained.

Samuel said," The county will buy you some."

"Thanks all the same," she said, "But they would ruin the leather." Samuel helped buckle them in and they left.

We crossed the bridge to the empty blue bungalow.

WE PICKED them up the next morning. Joshua's diaper was soaked through; Vivienne was crying; Kyle had a rash on his bottom. Samuel was nowhere to be found, having called me earlier to say, "It's Christmas Eve. You make the arrangements."

Cici complained, "They didn't eat very much of my mother's cooking."

"What did she make them?" Papa asked.

"Stuffed Jalapenos."

Papa frowned. "You know that they are still on baby food, right? After a reanastomosis, it may take years for him to eat regular food."

"Well, they better get used to it fast," she replied, and drove off in her car.

On a rainy Christmas Eve, we drove out to the Christmas by the Cove store, picked out an ornament with five bears in Christmas stockings, and personalized it with our names. Then we drove to Pasta Pomodoro for a chance to catch our breath and cherish the moment. We ordered bruschetta and steamed mussels and spaghetti and I toasted, "To the first Christmas with the triplets, as well as the future, whatever that may bring."

"We've got everything against us, you know," Papa growled. "Samuel and the county are going to do what's expedient. They're going to move them back in with a schizophrenic birth mother and a less-than-honest birth grandmother, in a very crowded studio apartment."

The bruschetta arrived. I took a bite, and, for once in my life, I wasn't hungry. "I know, I know. Look, we've got the losing hand in this, but we've got to keep playing. For their sake. Do you want to give up?"

"No, I wish I could. But I know the two of us, and I know we can't."

Papa (who never makes the toast) raised his glass and said, "To us then. Because we never stop fighting for what is right."

The pasta and clams arrived. "And if we lose?" I asked.

Papa replied, "I'm gonna get drunk for a month. And start smoking again. And you?"

"I don't know. Drive to North Dakota and become a cowboy. Fly to Alaska. I'll need to get away from California and all of the hopes and dreams I've spread beneath its feet. But I'll come back. Regrets?"

"No," Papa said, eating the one clam he would have for lunch. "We walked into this with our eyes open. I love these kids more than life itself, but we did what we could. And in the meantime, we hold on to the very last shred of hope."

I sang in church on Christmas Eve. When I went to Notre Dame, I sang with the Chapel Choir and they became family to me. To the present, I was still friends with people in that choir. One of the leading sopranos, Carol, was a devout atheist. When I asked why she sang Catholic music with us, she told me, "The experience is not about Catholicism; rather it is about the community, in the richness of blending my voice with all of you. That's all the heaven I will ever need."

A quarter of a century later, I liked being a bass again. I liked gathering to make a beautiful sound and I liked doing it in a church that emphasizes inclusivity over Christianity. As we sang "The Carol of the Bells," I cried because this family, no matter how fragile the status, was the most wonderful thing that I had ever been a part of. Brian listened, from the back of the church, with Kyle, Vivienne and Joshua all bundled up in red and green blankets. Kyle, of course, slept to whatever I sang.

On Christmas morning, we woke up to a bungalow filled with sunlight glowing through the white curtains. Nana and Santa had both conspired to fill any available space underneath the trees with gifts wrapped in bright blue, red and green. Papa and I helped the infants rip into their packages and that was all the joy I needed. What mattered was Kyle bopping a Fisher-Price star and laughing because he made the light turn on. Joshua got into Christmas more than the other two. While Vivienne stared and Kyle chewed on the corner of some gift paper,

Joshua gleefully ripped at packages, whether they were addressed to him or not. Most of the toys that Nana sent made noises, and he enjoyed that most of all. He especially loved playing with this Sesame Street figure of Oscar that yelled out, "I love trash!!" every ten seconds. Of course, the toy quickly lost its charm for me, but *de gustibus non disputandum est.*

Pop had mailed out teddy bears for the two boys, and a doll with a crocheted pink dress. There was a note, "Nurse Vivian made this doll a few years ago in case she ever had another granddaughter. Somewhere she knows that she does."

And, oh, yes, Santa had even filled Miss Grrrl's stocking with snausages.

New Year's Day 2004

Before talking about the last day of 2003, let me talk about the last day of 1968. A week or so after the tree decorating, South Ozone Park celebrated New Year's Eve. We went over to the McCaffery's and watched on the ancient black and white Zenith as Guy Lombardo counted down the clock. Times Square was less than fifteen miles away, yet none of us ever thought of going there. Instead we sat around with tin cans and spoons and the minute that the ball dropped, we ran outside into the snow, banging on pots. Joe McCaffery filmed us every year on his

Super 8 camera as the parents kissed and the little kids ran around sneaking sips of their mothers' highballs. Jeannie McCormick, the songbird of South Ozone Park, sang old Maguire Sisters hits, and my father sang Frank Sinatra songs. I dozed off while listening quietly on the couch, only to wake in my own bed the following morning.

Nurse Vivian used to be the last person on the block to take down the Christmas tree. The Caddens, McCormicks, and Carbones all raced to box up their plastic Christmas trees and get back to serious football. Peggy McCaffery, our next-door neighbor, was the only one in the neighborhood to get a real tree. They cut off a lot of branches to make it fit into their row house, making for an unnaturally square tree. She took all the tinsel off and left it for the garbage men to pick up on January 2nd. But Nurse Vivian always made us wait the full twelve days of Christmas. I felt like I was out of date with the rest of the kids, but Nurse Vivian said, "Oh, let everybody else rush through Christmas like they want to get it over with. We don't do that in our house. Now that everybody else is finished, I can sit back and enjoy my own tree."

"What are we waiting for?"

"The Feast of the Magi."

"The what?"

"January 6th is the Feast of the Magi. It is the day that the three wise men brought gifts for the little baby. Why would you want to take down your Christmas tree when you never know when three kings might stop in, and what gifts they might bring?"

Three kings never did stop by that house on Sutter Avenue, but on January 6 I packed up my clothespin ornaments as my mother unscrewed tree branches.

On the last day of 2003, we had three little magi in the nursery and they had each given me their own gift. Vivienne gave me that burpy little laugh she got every time I picked her up. As an extra bonus, she was teaching herself to sit up. Kyle gave me the weight gain that he needed and also had started hauling himself around the house just like the other two. None of them had reached the Waterford Crystal level yet, but it was just a matter of time.

And Joshua? Well, the developmental specialist came by that week and told us that the three kids were learning gross motor skills (pounding on things), and fine motor skills (pinching Daddy just as he was trying to diaper), but she was a little disappointed about their verbal skills. They all had managed the raspberry noise, but none of them were repeating vowel sounds. They should've been saying *gagagaga* or *pepepe* by this time. So we talked to them, and encouraged them, and yet they smiled inscrutably, saying nothing. The next night, Maureen and Uncle Jon came over to play bridge, and somehow during the course of this,

Joshua got to feeling ignored, so he crawled from the living room over to the dining room over to my chair, pulled at my shoelaces and started babbling, "Dada. Dada. Dada." Brian thought it was a nonsense syllable, but I knew better.

In terms of Christmas miracles, we were working on Uncle Tim. With his stomach problems he wasn't able to keep down any AIDS drugs. All the drug combinations were toxic. I compared the AIDS drugs to Drano; they might get at the disease, but they were hell on the plumbing. By now, Uncle Tim had lost over a hundred pounds and his viral load was 450,000. His T-cell count was at six. In reality, short of a miracle, he'd be lucky to see another Groundhog Day, let alone Christmas.

His doctor, just grasping at anything, put him on Trizivir. Trizivir is a combination of three different drugs in one horse pill that has to be taken twice daily. It was about the least effective AIDS therapy on the market, and prescribed mainly for homeless people who couldn't handle taking six or seven different AIDS drugs a day. Uncle Tim was eating it with ice cream and keeping it down. Miracles happened, at least for now; his viral load dropped from 450,000 to 2,200.

I was glad the tree was still up. The magi had always come, even if I hadn't always recognized the gift.

CHAPTER 11

Sadie Hawkins Day

February 15, 2004

T HIS WAS a very important weekend. On Thursday, February 12, San Francisco Mayor Gavin Newsom challenged eleven hundred years of discrimination by directing the city-county clerk to issue marriage licenses to same-sex couples. He asserted that the California Constitution's equal protection clause gave him authority to grant same-sex marriage licenses, proclaiming that "this is about bringing people together." This was the most crucial event in gay history since Stonewall. Hundreds of gay and lesbian couples flocked to City Hall in the next few days to get marriage certificates that might become illegal by Tuesday.

Yes, Tuesday. An army of right-wing Republicans worked over the weekend to steal our rights away again, and it was likely that they would get an injunction from the court after the President's Day holiday.

Instead of getting married, however, Papa and I ended up playing cribbage. We celebrated our nineteenth Valentine's Day by having a late-night supper of Progresso Chicken Tuscany soup while Miss Grrrl guarded the triplets. When discussing the possibility of getting married, Papa joked, "Simply put, I am not ready for another anniversary date to remember."

After all, we remember October 8th, the day we met; October 27, the day we started dating; April 6, the day we got Miss Grrrrl; and April 1, the day we brought the triplets home. We were well on the way to turning every date on the calendar year into a day to remember: the day that Papa won the Isadora Duncan Award, the day that I was awarded Deputy Sheriff of the Year, the day that Papa danced before the President of the United States, the day I got my first story published, the day that Miss Grrrrl had puppies. With each of these celebrations, we had called out to our community of friends to come witness what we had done.

One of our more splendid dates was September 19, 1987, when, in a driving New York City rain, the kind that made the city glisten, we had our commitment ceremony. It was the rainiest day either of us ever remembered. We invited fifty of our friends and family to join us in a bar in Chelsea, decorated in white roses and calla lilies.

A Roman Catholic priest, Father Mariano, officiated. Tony lit a candle and passed the flame to another candle and soon all of our friends held a little bit of fire, and in the light of that fire, Grandpa Jerry read the part of the Bible where it said David loved Jonathan above all others. Cousin Rita read from Corinthians that "without love, I am but a bell clanging or a cymbal clashing." Amanda read from *The Little Prince*, the part where the Fox leaves the Little Prince with this wisdom: "It is the time that you have wasted on your rose that has made your rose so important."

And then Papa and I promised that, "...like the circle of the rings, we will always turn back to each other, and like the gold of the rings we will always hold each other as precious." It was the light of that community that our love has reflected for all of these years.

We have let our light shine and we have changed our little corner of the planet.

That weekend, the triplets took priority over rushing out to City Hall to get a certificate in front of a group of anonymous strangers. After a cast on Vivienne's arm, hernia surgery for Joshua and heart valve surgery for Kyle, as well as a reanastomosis of the ileum and physical therapy and a few too many trips to the emergency room, the three children were healthy and happy. All three sat up, stood with support, and most importantly, said, "Dada.

Dada. Dada. Dada. Dada." Kyle occasionally punctuated that with a trill. Vivienne giggled afterward.

We took the children over to Oakland for a visit with Cici. The boys were hungry, so I handed Cici a bottle and asked her if she wanted to feed Joshua. She held him, but kept getting distracted by her cell phone. He cried, and Cici asked, "Does he always do this? Why can't he feed himself?"

We could smell that Vivienne's diaper was full. "Do you want to change her?" I asked.

Cici smirked at me, "I don't do diapers. These kids better get trained fast."

Samuel, our social worker, came over to visit us. He sat nervously in our kitchen, scribbling notes in his binder. Without much introduction, he said, "I wanted to tell you that I have spoken with the social worker for the county, and we have come up with a plan. A hearing has been scheduled for March 9th, and on that day, the county intends to sever reunification services and move the triplets in with Cici's mother."

"But Cici lives with the mother," I protested. "And you yourself said that Cici was a danger to the children."

"If you fight this," he continued, blankly, "the agency will not support you, and you can be certain that Cici will make sure that you never see the children again. The county is paying for her lawyer, and you two will go broke long before you will ever see those children again."

After a year of three a.m. feedings, diaper changes at dawn, ileostomy bag changes every five hours, and all that rocking in the rocking chair, it looked like it might be time to give up the fight. We didn't say this to each other simply because we didn't know how to say it.

Uncle Jon and Aunt Lori came over to play cribbage on Sunday, a game we had played together for almost ten years. We don't play for money, but we do play for the ownership of the Cribbage Queen Ornament, a pottery ornament that I made years ago, and whose ownership defines the best cribbage-playing skills in California. Papa and I were always partners, and Uncle Jon and Aunt Lori were married in the eyes of the cribbage board.

We played cribbage at the kitchen table (Nurse Vivian was right) because we needed to remember that no matter what, life continued. We still had friends and we still had each other. And there was always cribbage.

We held our own in the first two games, but in the third, Papa, the ace cribbage player in the group, added an eight to a count of thirty, thus making the count thirty-eight. If you don't know how to play cribbage, just know that this is a very silly thing to do.

Aunt Lori asked, "What's going on?" she counted her 24 point crib and gathered the cards up to shuffle.

I replied, "We're getting to the end here. We've already

spent a couple thousand dollars on legal fees and we're in debt up to our noses, and we don't want to lose the chance to see the kids ever again."

Kyle whimpered from his bedroom. I went in to look at him. "But," Papa added, "we feel that placing these wonderful children with a grandmother who has been lying about living with her schizophrenic drug-using daughter is just wrong. We have seen the mother shake the babies. We have seen the mother walk out on the babies. We have seen the mother show up to pick up the kids in a car with no car seats."

I continued, "Dr. Halberg gave us a very strict diet of pre-digested proteins for Kyle because he is missing a part of his intestine. She forbade juice, among other foods, and she informed the birth mother of this in both English and Spanish. Nevertheless, every time Kyle comes back from visiting her he has diarrhea. When we finally demanded that the social worker check into this, he reported that the grandmother had been feeding him juice or soda every time."

Aunt Lori dealt the cards out. "What choices do you have?"

I said, "It would hurt like hell to see them go, but the county is sending everything they can against us."

Neither Aunt Lori nor Uncle Jon hesitated a minute. With one voice, they said, "Keep fighting. If you need money, we'll find it."

Years ago in our commitment ceremony, we had vowed that we would always fight for what is right. Our friends and family witnessed that promise. That was exactly what we were going to do. We were going to fight this until the very, very, very last proceeding. Through our lawyer, we hired an attachment expert and we were challenging every assumption that the social workers had made. Our lawyer was actually more hopeful than we were, but then again, at $275 an hour, he was paid to be hopeful. He was filing officially for *de facto* parental status for us. This status would at least give us the opportunity to go to the hearing on March 9th and present our case. We could then request that someone monitor the family to make sure that the kids were protected.

About four of our friends were pregnant at the time and all four of these women would make great mothers. But at times it was a harsh reminder that we were not birth parents. Papa and I knew that our path would not be easy. We paid a price to be different. I liked to think that the universe gave us these challenges because we could surpass them. I also liked to think that these kids would be with us forever. There had to be a reason that these wonderful children were with us now. If there was anything to this kismet business, then every ileostomy bag we replaced worked off a little negative karma.

If there was a lesson in all of this, maybe it was the lesson of learning how to play a hand of cribbage when we knew we were losing. We still didn't know what to say but we did know that the story was not over. We knew we were approaching an ending but we didn't know what the ending would be.

We wanted to think that this was one of those Star Trek "Kobayashi Maru" moments when the Klingon Birds of Prey, the Romulan Warships, and the Borg Cubes are all pointed at the Enterprise, and although we have no shields or phasers, at the very last second, Scottie whips up a miracle and Kirk smiles craftily, knowing that he holds the winning hand of Fizz Bin.

We wanted to think that what we were doing with the triplets was more important than just making history.

February 26, 2004

Despite my love of show tunes, I'd never seen *Li'l Abner*. But since my favorite actress in the whole world, Julie Newmar (aka Catwoman), got her start as Stupefyin' Jones in the musical, and of course, Uncle Tim had once played Evil Eye Fleagle, (typecasting at its best), he taught me a little about the plot. During the last act, the cast celebrates Sadie Hawkins day. Sadie Hawkins was the homeliest gal in all of Dogpatch, and her father, Mayor Hezekiah Hawkins, ordered that on February 29th, all the

women, including Stupefyin' Jones and Daisy Mae, would
have a foot race where the fastest one gets to hunt down
the man she wants, namely Li'l Abner.

At Notre Dame, we had a few Sadie Hawkins Day
Dances where the women asked the men out, but the idea
never really caught on because, well, it was Notre Dame.
It was also because February 29th only comes once every
four years and even if the dance went well for you as a
freshman, by the time the next Sadie Hawkins day came
around, you'd no longer be eligible to attend.

Here in San Francisco, it struck me that we ought to
have the gay equivalent of Sadie Hawkins Day, a day where
gay men can ask a straight man out to musical theater, the
symphony or the opera, and the straight man would have
to go rather than staying home and watching basketball.
This way, every straight guy would have a queer eye at
least once every four years. And this way, every straight
woman would have one night where they knew that their
husband/boyfriend was actually out getting a little culture,
and would come back better mannered, maybe even with
a good haircut and a manicure.

It would probably never pass — but this was San Francisco, where Gavin Newsom made anything possible.

Sadie Hawkins Day didn't catch on for a lot of reasons, one of which might be because the Catholics had
cornered the market on February celebrations. But the

other February holidays lacked a certain pizzazz. No one did anything more exciting than wake up at dawn to watch Punxatawnie Phil see his shadow on Groundhog Day. Big Whoop. And who even bakes a cherry pie for Washington's Birthday? The department stores maybe, but not the people. Still, the Catholics had Mardi Gras. Since the holiday literally means Fat Tuesday, I did my best to ignore carbohydrate and fat counts for the day. Nana was visiting, so I roasted pork with onions, carrots, and broccoli. This was after a three-dessert lunch. But I might as well have a good excuse for my expanding waistline, and what the heck, maybe I would indeed give up something for Lent.

The next day dawned and Papa, who is really good at giving up food, asked me what I was giving up. "Skydiving and cotton candy," I replied, a stock line that Pop had used on Nurse Vivian for the fifty-four years of their marriage. Since I had indeed gone skydiving, I was tempted to pick chocolate or cheeseburgers, since I knew that I really didn't need those anyway, and that way I could use the next six weeks to lose a little of my PFA (Paulson Fat Ass.)

Faith is a wobbly thing, and with that I aimed for something a little higher than my waistline. For Lent, I would *try* to give up my anger at the birth family of the triplets. I would *try* to give up my anger at Cici who took drugs, didn't cooperate with the doctors, never set herself up with a psychiatrist, and ended up getting three very sweet children very sick. I would *try* to give up my anger that the grandmother didn't step in and get her daughter the help she so clearly needed. I would *try* to give up my anger that the grandmother stated that she would triple her income if she convinced the court to give her these kids.

Somewhere in the city, Uncle Tim was doing his best Yoda imitation: *Do or do not. There is no try.*

This was tough stuff. I had little faith, and the courts and county were attacking what little was left. But rather than dwell on the possibility of losing the triplets, I chose to follow the lesson of Saint Theresa. You would think the saints had the faith thing all figured out, and all they had to do was muster a little of it to chase snakes out of Ireland or deliver toys on Christmas Eve. But Saint Theresa was different. She actually had very little faith, and she chose to live her life *as if* she believed in faith. That belief gave her purpose.

Centuries later I had chosen my own kind of faith, that deep down there was a reason to love and to make beauty.

I asked myself over and over again if Papa and I were fools to take in these triplets, and the only answer that I came up with is that when the social worker called that April Fool's Day, we did the right thing. And now, we needed to take care of these kids as best we could, and give them whatever love we could, and hope that the love was enough. So I was *trying* to give up my anger. That didn't mean I'd stop fighting. No, this was a fight to the end. I was just *trying* to go through all of this with as much respect and as much honor as I could for Cici and the grandmother, while protecting the triplets in whatever way I could.

I spoke with our lawyer that day and he said, "The court replied that they will consider the motion for de facto parent status on March 9th, as well as the proposed change in placement. This means, in effect, that the court has to make a decision about whether we know enough about the triplets to present an authoritative opinion and ultimately, whether or not we get the opportunity to present our side. The hearing will be closed to the public, meaning that all of the friends who offered to come won't be able to attend."

"So far this does not sound hopeful," I replied.

The attorney added, "I will make a motion to contest the county's recommendation in a special hearing. If we get that hearing, I will present evidence of our ability to parent the children effectively, which means letting the judge know how much these kids are loved by your community."

Two nights later, Kyle finally joined the ranks of persons on the planet with teeth. Or at least a tooth. We were keeping Orajel in business. Joshua, the competitive

Kevin Fisher-Paulson

brother, then had two teeth, and Vivienne, never a girl to be outdone, just finished growing her first upper, for a grand total of three. All three kids crawled now, and stood up if leaning against something. Kyle was a little slower than the other two, but was turning out to be the sly one. He watched Vivienne and Joshua through their trial and error process for weeks, stumbling into a standing position, only to lose their balance and go *bonk* against the wooden floor. But Kyle watched and waited, and after he saw all the mistakes of the other two, just crawled over to the couch one day and pulled himself up. He listened to Joshua and Vivienne make noises like "Geeeeeeeee" and "Dadadadadada" and "RRRRRRR" and then, just as I picked him up to feed him his evening bottle, he looked right up at me and said, "I love you, Daddy!"

Papa insisted that it sounded more like "Giguhgoogagee" but Papa was well into his middle years, and his hearing had started to go, poor thing.

When you get the chance, have a great Sadie Hawkins Day. Chase and catch the little Abner of your dreams. Someday, you may even be able to marry him.

CHAPTER 12

Sunset in San Francisco

March 9, 2004

OUR NEIGHBOR Dorla invited us over for dinner on Sunday for an early celebration of the triplets' birthday. This was only the second dinner invitation that the triplets had gotten. Thus she earned a free upgrade to *Aunt Dorla*. (The first invitation was to Uncle Jon's house, and he served them a delicious *consommé de Enfamil*, followed by a casserole of smashed peas.) We took Aunt Dorla up on the dinner invitation, figuring what the heck, if she wanted all five of us over for the evening, then she was welcome to have us.

Dinner was set for six o'clock but Vivienne had a hard time deciding on an outfit. She had a pantsuit but that seemed too casual. She looked good in her purple dress that she had regrettably outgrown the week before. Finally, she settled on a simple pink cotton dress with an Empire waist and bloomers. We arrived half an hour late but Vivienne was still the belle of the ball, casually mingling on one lap and then another. As a surprise, Aunt Dorla invited pretty much the entire neighborhood, saying merely, "Their first birthday party."

Joshua sat with his Aunt Lori for the most part, but Kyle made new friends. Tita Ann, another neighbor, walked into the dining room with him, and I could see that he was using his two tiny little teeth to saw into a cracker, getting crumbs all over. From the smile on his face, you would have thought that the cracker was topped with caviar.

The highlight of the evening came as we sang around the piano. Quentin, Tita Ann's Uncle, had brought along a Broadway songbook. The minute Quentin played *"You'll be swell, you'll be great! Gonna have the whole world on a plate!"* Kyle reached out for me and started clapping.

As we finished that song, Quentin launched into the Happy Birthday song, and in came Aunt Dorla with a huge cake with three candles on it. Instead of blowing out the candles, Joshua simply stuck his fist into the cake.

Before I could even grab a slice, Quentin played "Sunrise, Sunset" from *Fiddler on the Roof,* and I got a little sentimental singing, *"Is this the little girl I carried? Is this the little boy at play?"* After all, I just might never see the kids grow up.

Uncle Tim walked me out to Aunt Dorla's yard. He lit

a cigarette. I had to say it: "You know those can kill you, right?"

"Honey, I'm dying of AIDS and your little drama is crashing around our ears. Have a piece of cake, and let's go easy on ourselves for one night."

The wind rustled above the pine trees.

"By the way, I made you a gift," he continued, handing me a small narrow package wrapped in purple tissue paper. I opened it. Three candles were decorated with gold sparkles in symbols that he had taught me were runes. "I know that you don't believe in this Wiccan business, and lately it has been hard to believe in anything else. So I'm casting a very specific spell. Once you light these, you, me, and Brian are forever linked to the triplets. A part of our energy, wherever they are, will always keep them safe."

"Can you afford that energy?" I asked, looking at his thinning build, his burning eyes.

"What else was I gonna use it for? I'm going fast. I might as well teach you a lesson or two about faith. And it's a lot more festive than that statue of Saint Jude you keep in the china cabinet."

THE NEXT afternoon our social worker, Samuel, came over, sat in the kitchen, pulled out his notebook and said, "You need to be prepared for separation. Once you lose this hearing, I will pick up the children by four."

The bottom fell out. The *ifs* kept tumbling around in my head. *What if this is the last time that I take them out in the stroller? What if this is the last time that Vivienne giggles at me?*

It had been a beautiful spring day with a stunning sunset that turned the sky bright gold and red. As Joshua, Kyle, Vivienne, and I sat on the porch, watching the turquoise sky turn indigo, I got it. This might be our last sunset together. So I let go. I stopped worrying about the hearing and the laundry and the job and the car payments and the lawyer's fees. If this was to be my last sunset with them, we would enjoy every color in the sky.

As the last traces of scarlet settled in the west, I lit the three candles from Uncle Tim. And I told God that if there is a God, then I wanted *this* miracle. The stars appeared in the upper window of the porch. It was an exceptionally clear night, and I told the children that we would make a wish on each of the three stars of Orion's belt.

PAPA, UNCLE JON, and I arrived at eight-thirty in the morning for the hearing, which was set for nine o'clock. Our lawyer arrived at eight-fifty-nine. The other lawyers strolled in at around nine-thirty. There was a lawyer for the birth mother, paid for by the state of California. There was Ms. Wong, a lawyer for the county of Alameda, paid for by the state of California. There was a lawyer for the three children, paid for by the state of California. Then

there was our lawyer, paid for by the Fisher-Paulsons. Since I paid my taxes, I was, in effect, paying for all four of these lawyers to argue about a truth that I knew in my heart: the children belonged with us.

Our lawyer asked the baby's lawyer, "Can I speak with you for a minute?" He just shook his head and walked over to Cici's lawyer. The birth mother and birth grandmother showed up. Cici grumbled, "I hope this doesn't take all day. I'm getting my hair done today."

We waited another expensive hour and finally our lawyer walked up to the baby's lawyer and said, "You're listening to a lawyer who has never even met these kids. Don't you think you should ask the foster parents?"

The baby's lawyer walked up to us and asked, "Do you have any concerns about the triplets moving in with the birth family?"

I said, "Yes, I am concerned. Do you really think it is wise to move these fragile children into a house with a woman with history of psychiatric disorder and drug abuse? A woman who shakes the baby when no one is watching? A woman who walks out on the children when she gets bored?"

The lawyer was shocked. "Why isn't any of this in the social worker's report?"

"Maybe because we have had fourteen different social workers on this case. None of them have been around long enough to put the points together. Or maybe because someone is leaving something out."

They called the case in. The county lawyer, Cici's lawyer, and the baby's lawyer were in a full court press. The judge, Judge Gee, was nice. He softly rapped the gavel and said, "This is a difficult case, made difficult by the love I have seen from these two men for the children, balanced against the wishes expressed by the birth grandmother."

The baby's lawyer, perhaps a little thrown off by my speech, said, "I agree to move the children in with the grandmother only if there is a thirty-day follow-up. In the meantime, we should schedule a 26 hearing [which would sever the mother's birthrights]."

In order to make the grandmother the guardian, there would have to be a 26 hearing. Judge Gee said, "Clearly the mother is in denial. She cannot be considered in any motion at this time to re-unite the children with the birth mother, but the grandmother could be considered, provided she can provide a separate home."

Ned got up and said, "If it please the court, I have introduced a motion for *de facto* parent status and I would like the judge to rule on that issue." The other lawyers riffled through their paperwork with concerned looks.

The judge asked "What motion?"

The clerk of the court handed him the motion to institute *de facto* status.

The baby's lawyer said, "I never got that motion."

The judge looked down at his paperwork. He said, "Well, the court paperwork indicates that this court mailed you a copy on February 25th."

The baby's lawyer said, "I never got it."

Cici's lawyer said, "I never got it."

Samuel, the social worker, looked sheepish and said, "I got it."

Ned started talking fast and furious, pointing out, "No one else in this court has a continuous history with the kids. The baby's lawyer has never seen the kids. Cici's lawyer has never seen the kids. The social worker has seen the kids at fifteen-minute intervals once a month."

The judge read through the statement and said, "Well, given these new facts, I cannot allow these children to be moved out of a place that they are obviously prospering in at this time. But since none of the lawyers have read their mail, I will need to set a hearing for the *de facto* status before I can set a hearing for the placement of the children."

In other words, we did not win the day — but we most certainly did not lose. We were being considered for *de facto* status, which would give us some legal standing. A day before, I'd thought the kids might be gone forever, but now we had one flimsy hope: that the justice system would indeed perform justice.

Ned took us to a Starbucks later, and said, "This is just

about the best outcome we could have hoped for. The bad news is that *now* the county will do anything they can to stop us."

The next hearing was set for March 19. Papa would be dancing in Sheboygan so Uncle Jon volunteered to step in as *de facto* uncle.

I drove home. Vivienne was smiling, playing with her doll from Nurse Vivian. The boys busied themselves chewing the stars that Nana had sent them from Fisher-Price.

The candles still flickered on the porch.

CHAPTER 13

Once More Into the Breach, Dear Fellows

March 20, 2004

WORKING ON Nurse Vivian's logic that you should always get dressed up when you meet professional people, I put on a good suit and a silk tie for the *de facto* parent hearing. For my mother, a professional person was anybody with a title in front of their name. We Paulsons were the only boys on the block who had to wear a collared shirt to go to the dentist. She also insisted on dressing up to get on trains and airplanes, and to this day I find myself putting on dress shoes before I get into a taxi.

The triplets were still asleep as we left, except for Joshua, proud of himself in his green velour dragon pajama, roaring at me. I kissed him goodbye, then leaned over the cribs to kiss the other two.

Uncle Jon and I arrived half an hour early and sat in the

lobby, unable to make small talk, unable to read. I was the Peter Pan of jurisprudence. I had never even served on a jury before and I had always thought of the law as a grown-up activity somewhat beyond my ken. So there I sat in a courthouse lobby thinking about how much I wanted my mother there with me to tell me that everything was going to be all right.

Our attorney, Ned Summerfield, arrived and then, as all the lawyers and social workers approached, I grew up.

We filed into the courtroom, the bailiff called the court to order, and in walked Judge Gee. He started the proceedings with the announcement: "The court will hear two matters, the *de facto* status of Mr. Fisher and Mr. Paulson and the matter of the placement of the children."

In terms of the first issue, he asked the birth attorney if he had any objections. He did not. He asked the county attorney, Ms. Wong, if she had any objections. She did. She stated, "This is a sneaky way to insert their opinions into the proceedings. What do these two know about real families anyway?"

Judge Gee replied, "Given the time these two have spent with the children and the level of care that they have provided, I am granting *de facto* parent status." A small victory, as the status did little for us except provide the opportunity to present information to the court.

Cici arrived, wearing an Old Navy t-shirt, jeans and

flip flops. To her mother she said a little loudly, "I'm busy this week. I wish we could just get this over with. Why do I have to keep coming?"

Ms. Wong stood up, tapping her fingers, manicured in red this morning. "If it please your honor, the point is moot if you will just rule on the second issue, the movement of the children."

Judge Gee nodded, paused and then asked, "Does anyone have any objection to the motion?"

Ned stood up and said, "Your honor, I have never seen the motion."

Judge Gee shook his head and asked Ms. Wong, "Why have you not provided a copy to counsel?"

Ms. Wong smirked, "I didn't think he needed one. These people have nothing to do with the children —"

Through clenched teeth, Judge Gee said "Give him a copy immediately."

Ms. Wong handed the document to a very nice bailiff, a man a few years older than me, who handed a copy to the Judge and then to Ned. This is what the report said: "Because of the mother's mental illness, it is unlikely that she will ever be able to take care of the children. The county therefore recommends placement with the birth grandmother."

Judge Gee asked, "Isn't it unusual for the county to move the children into a home where there is someone with a mental illness?"

To which Ms. Wong responded, "I feel that the children would receive the minimum level of care. The grandmother has made strides."

He then asked her, "Do you mean to tell me that you recommend moving the children from a place where they get *excellent* care to a place where they get *minimum standards enough* care?"

She said, "Yes, your honor." Then seeing that the judge did not like that answer, she added, "I mean that the birth family has made excellent strides and I think that eventually they will provide an equivalent level of care." The birth mother pulled out an audio player, and the bailiff walked over and told her she could not play music in the court.

Ned interceded, asking, "Since the mother is not a viable option as stated by documentation, would the court consider alternative placement for the children?"

Judge Gee, scratching his chin, asked, "Can you cite any cases?"

Ned cited cases. Then the other lawyers cited some other counter cases, at which point Judge Gee said, "I need a recess." We shuffled outside. I did not have a candy bar. I did not have a latte. Somewhere in Wisconsin, Papa was not having a cigarette, waiting for me to call.

While we were talking, Ms. Wong came out with a

Kevin Fisher-Paulson

grim smile into the hallway and said, "I'm calling the judge back from his recess. We're making an alternate proposal and both Cici's attorney as well as the baby's attorney agree with me."

The bailiff brought the court back in order. Judge Gee entered the chamber, frowning at Ms. Wong, "You're making a counter offer, as if this were buying a car?"

Ms. Wong closed her leather briefcase and stood up, "Your honor, we have changed our earlier request. We move to move the children back in to the care of the birth mother."

These were the same people who had just said an hour previous that the mother was mentally ill.

If judges ever gape, then Judge Gee gaped. He looked directly at Ms. Wong. "After everything you have previously submitted, are you prepared to bring witnesses to contradict what you have already said about the mother's mental health?"

Ms. Wong nodded firmly, "Of course it will take some time to find the appropriate witnesses and prepare their testimony."

Judge Gee scowled. "It has been my experience that testimony that is *prepared* in advance is rarely as truthful as spontaneous testimony."

Ms. Wong said, "Nevertheless, I will produce these witnesses." She snapped her Luis Vuitton briefcase shut.

Judge Gee said, "This case will take at least two days to try, probably three."

Ms. Wong smiled, "Then I would like the authority to place the children wherever the county saw best until your honor can decide their future."

Judge Gee shook his head, "I suppose that I need to trust the county to make the right decision."

Ms. Wong smiled, and the baby's attorney smiled and Cici's attorney smiled, and I looked at our lawyer.

He said, "Your honor, in how many days does the county intend to move these children in with the birth family?"

She drew her lips in closely and said, "Thirty days."

Judge Gee, realizing that he had been had, said, "Well, in that case, I will rule on the issue. You will have a maximum of seventy-two hours for the birth family to see the children until the end of these proceedings. And I am ordering that all discovery in this case be turned over to Ned Summerfield."

Cici's attorney objected, saying that the psychological history of the mother was a matter of privacy, at which point the baby's attorney said, "Well, I read it, so it's hardly private."

Judge Gee said, tightly, "I will make a ruling about that next week."

Ms. Wong tapped her table with scarlet fingernails and

said, "These foster parents have no standing in the court. They are not eligible to adopt."

Ms. Wong and Judge Gee stared at each other for a cold minute and then he said, "*I* will make a ruling on how much standing the *de facto* parents have next week. All of you (looking at the three lawyers) have until noon on Monday to submit a brief about the issue. This court is adjourned."

The birth grandmother sneered at me as I walked out.

Ned took us to Starbucks again. I had a decaf latté made with scalded whipping cream and caramel syrup. Even on a bad day, this is better than a shot of scotch.

After my first sip, Ned started, "The grandmother has no rights in the hearing. The *de facto* parents have no rights in this hearing. The only people with rights are the triplets and the birth mother. And it is almost impossible to get the children if the court rules that the mother is fit to take care of the children."

Ned continued, "In getting *de facto* status we have won the battle, but the war has become very, very difficult to win. If the county is now changing its official opinion of the mother's mental health status, we face even more difficult odds to beat. After all, the social workers control the reports that get to the court."

"And how will this work?" I asked, the latté growing colder in my hand.

He estimated: "There will be at least twenty-four hours of trial, sixteen hours of preparations, and four hours preparing briefs, all on top of the time that I have already spent on the case. In addition, we need to pay for the attachment expert. The hearing will start on Friday." In essence, he told us that keeping hope alive had become very expensive.

Nurse Vivian used to say, "Spend all your money now before your kids think of it as an inheritance." We would press on.

I called Samuel to let him know what had happened in court and to say, "I will drive the kids over to the agency so that the birth family can pick them up for the seventy-two hour visit."

Samuel said, "I stopped by to see the children today. The girl kept crying and calling for 'Daddy.'"

The odds were against us. The county was against us. Three out of four lawyers were against us. But I knew this much to be true: Cici was mentally ill and her behavior would put the children in danger. I needed to fight for the safety of the only three people who thought of me as "Daddy."

This case had taken on an importance way beyond Papa and me. This had become a story about tilting at windmills, about doing whatever you needed to do to keep hope, and maybe faith, alive. Perhaps most heartening was the effect the story had on the cynics.

My friend Dave, a devout agnostic, asked if the prayers of agnostics counted, and I answered that they count twice: once because of the prayer and twice because of the risk.

CHAPTER 14

Ten Thousand Miles

Hope springs eternal in the human breast;
Man never is, but always to be blest:
The soul, uneasy and confin'd from home,
Rests and expatiates in a life to come.
-ALEXANDER POPE,
An Essay on Man, Epistle I, 1733

March 26, 2004

NURSE VIVIAN drank highballs whenever Frank Cadden, one of our Irish neighbors, threw a party. And Frank Cadden made a mean highball. He threw parties for all sorts of occasions, mainly come-as-you-are parties, which were pretty risqué for an Irish neighborhood in South Ozone Park. On a few occasions, Peggy McCaffery showed up in her baby doll pajamas and night robe, but the other mothers, including Nurse Vivian, usually took the time to put on makeup and a cocktail dress. Aunt Mildred once showed up for one of these impromptu parties with a pair of plastic buttocks she found in a novelty store, surrounded by a toilet seat. She kept telling everyone, "This is as come-as-you-are as I get."

Frank Cadden threw a baby shower for Queenie, the collie owned by the McCormicks, who found herself in a family way after a less than discreet run-in with Max, a German Shepherd owned by the Mallowitzes, the only Jewish family on the block.

Sally, Frank's second wife after his first wife Ida had died, had a touch of brogue, reminding you that she was straight off the farm in County Cork. There was a certain ritual to Frank and Sally's parties. After the first round of drinks, just like on New Year's Eve, my father sang "There is a Tavern in the Town." After the second round, Jeannie McCormick sang old Maguire Sisters hits. After the third round of highballs, my mother stood up and recited poetry. She had a gift for memorizing verse, and her favorite was called "The Face on the Barroom Floor" by Hugh D'Arcy. When Nurse Vivian died two years ago, Earl put pinochle cards in the coffin; Donald put in rosary beads and blackberry brandy. I added a copy of the poem. Her other favorite poem was a short one from Alexander Pope which she never credited. Thanks to Google, all mysteries have been solved in the 21st century.

Frank Cadden got sick unexpectedly in his mid-forties. Cancer, I think, but grownups did not discuss sick adults with children. When the doctors told him that his time was up, he invited my mother, who worked in the hospital, up to his room. He then asked, "Vivian, recite one of your poems to me."

"Oh, Frank, I only do that at your parties."

"Vivian," he said, pointing at his hospital gown, "This is as come-as-you-are as I get."

She launched into, *"Twas a balmy summer evening, and a goodly crowd was there, which well nigh filled the barroom, on the corner of the square ..."* which to my knowledge, was the only time she recited poetry while sober.

Frank died the next day. My mother went out that night, after helping Sally with the funeral arrangements, bought a living room couch and a Zenith color TV, the first color TV in all of South Ozone Park. She took down the stepladder and paint brushes and announced, "Life is too short for black and white."

About ten years ago, when I was working in County Jail # 3 in old San Bruno, I started memorizing poems. The inmates got locked in at nine o'clock at night and most of the other deputies sat around eating or playing poker while I walked up and down the tiers reciting poems to myself and occasionally to the inmates. Some thought I was crazy; some thought I was rapping. I don't drink highballs so most of my friends had never heard this stuff.

The blue bungalow was unbearably empty with the triplets gone for three days. I cleaned the house compulsively, washed all their clothes, and ironed Vivienne's dresses. Even the bark of the dogs seemed emptier. Reciting poems again helped a little.

On Monday, I went to A Better Way, our foster care agency, to pick up the kids from their visit with Cici. Samuel had said, "Meet me at three o'clock." Just before I left, he called and said, "Make it four instead." I agreed, since this gave me time to pick up Papa. After his rehearsal we drove across the bridge to Berkeley. We arrived a little after four. The children weren't there.

Samuel said, "Well, I wanted to meet with you first, and so I told the birth family not to come until four-thirty."

We went to his office.

He said, "Well, I just left a nasty message on your message machine, but I guess that you can ignore it now."

Papa, who has always had better instincts than me, said quietly, "What do you mean?"

Samuel rolled his eyes, caressed the cross on his chest and said, "What I mean is that I called Ms. Wong, and I volunteered to testify against you in court." The room got darker. "I've talked with my pastor at length, and we agree that it is much better for the children to be with the mother than with a same-sex couple."

I asked, "Samuel, you told us that the mother was mentally ill and unstable."

He answered, "She may be, but she will still provide a better home for the kids. I am prepared to testify in court that you two never understood reunification in the first place and that you fail to understand the cultural context in which the children lived."

"That's a lie." Papa's voice reached that dangerous whisper level. "Kevin speaks more Spanish than Cici. Beyond that the children are half Mexican/half Pakistani, and as far as I can see, no one has said anything about the children's Far Eastern heritage."

Samuel touched the cross one more time, put his hands on the desk, "Doesn't matter. They will at least have some culture, and some morals with her. Something two gay men could never do." The doorbell rang.

The birth grandmother was at the door, "My daughter couldn't make it. I'm double-parked over there, so could you hurry?" Samuel stayed long enough to see the children out of the car, then left.

Kyle's diaper was wet. Vivienne's diaper was wet, and her dress had food all down the front. Joshua and Vivienne were crying, and Kyle gave me that serious look. I changed diapers and loaded the kids into the car, while Papa left a scathing message with Erica, Samuel's supervisor. We drove across the Bridge to the bungalow. Miss Grrrl and

Wolfcub barked their greetings.

Erica called us back the following day. She said, "Your feelings must be really hurt. I'm sorry."

"Yes, Erica, but that solves nothing."

"I'd like to arrange a mediation. Can you come over tonight?"

I looked at Papa, and he nodded. We didn't really have a choice. We drove over the bridge again.

The office at A Better Way was quiet and empty, as if clearing the stage for our drama. We walked into Erica's office, lit with only one lamp. Erica sat behind a desk. Samuel sat in a chair, dressed in a button down shirt with that cross again. Papa and I sat down on the couch.

Samuel coughed and said, "I guess that I'll begin. You should know that I've been working against you for two months, but that Erica knew nothing about it."

Erica's eyes grew wide. She breathed in quickly. Papa closed his eyes. I growled, "You did what?"

"Well, I haven't been telling you everything. I know people like you. I tell you one thing, and you'll go and tell your lawyer, and before you know it those triplets would be condemned to the kind of life you offer. So I started calling Ms. Wong, and letting her know that in my opinion the birth mother was doing just fine —"

"But you barely saw her," Papa charged. "On the few occasions that she showed up, you left early."

"Nevertheless, my heart told me the truth," he said, patting the damn cross again. "And I told Ms. Wong that you have been obstructing reunification. It is my duty to make sure that these kids go back to a wholesome family."

"So you think that using crack makes a woman wholesome?"

Erica picked up her pen and started writing, saying, "I have never seen this happen in all my years of social work."

I was incensed. I asked, "Samuel, do you realize that you are advocating for moving the kids in with a mentally ill, abusive mother?"

Samuel smiled a tight smile, and said, "I admit that the mother does not have *all* the skills to raise the children. But she is a woman."

Erica asked him, "Do you understand the concept of concurrent planning?"

He shook his head and was silent.

"You have betrayed us," I seethed. "I've ignored your rudeness all this time, but now I see. You've been lying to us all this time."

Samuel nodded his head and admitted, "Yes, I have lied to you. I was frustrated, and what do you think you deserved anyway? You can't make babies so you steal them."

Erica raised her voice, "Samuel, frustration is no excuse for rudeness. What you have done has put this whole agency at risk."

Papa stood up, "I am more angry than I have ever been in my life. You have undermined everything that we have worked for in the past twelve months."

Samuel countered, "Yes, I have undermined you. I want these children to go back to the birth family, no matter what."

And all at once it made sense. Our case had been going very well until the point that Samuel walked in on us as we were talking to our lawyer. He listened to our discussion, where we talked about the fact that if the triplets moved in with the birth grandmother, then they would be exposed to what Cici did. We had discussed asking for *de facto* parent status so that someone would be watching out for the children. The next day, the county knew what our strategy was as well.

In the meantime, the judge ruled that he would hear all issues, the first being the mother's ability to parent. We had access to discovery, but he had sealed all records about the mother's psychological history. How do you prove that a woman is crazy when you are not allowed to read anything about the woman being crazy?

But the case continued. Ned spent the entire week preparing a defense while we looked for witnesses. We spent a few days trying to find people who could testify that schizophrenics do not spontaneously recover from methamphetamine, cocaine, alcohol, and haldol abuse, and that being placed in "the rubber room" six times in four years matters.

Erica called to say, "I fired Samuel."

But the damage was done. Although Samuel had lied to the county, his lies were in the official court documentation. We asked the agency to print a retraction. They were considering the request, but time was short.

Hope was still alive. If nothing else we had truth on our side. There had to be something said for truth.

For a moment I was back in the car, driving my mother to the airport, talking about adopting children: "Skydiving and tattoos weren't crazy enough? Two gay men playing house. Take a vacation. There is just too much heartbreak in raising children."

I'd like to think that Nurse Vivian had had a change of heart since passing to the other side. I'd like to think that she was asking St. Peter if he ever heard a poem called "The Face on the Barroom Floor." I'd like to think that she was proud of little Vivienne playing with the crocheted doll that she had made years ago for a theoretical granddaughter. I'd like to think that she was sitting there with Frank Cadden sipping highballs, watching color TV on her Zenith and saying to the Powers-that-Be, "Hey, you know what? My son has had enough bad luck. Would it hurt for you to give him a break once in a while?"

PAPA, THE TRIPLETS, and I were in the big blue Saturn Vue yesterday when I noticed that the odometer was at 9,999. We kept driving for what seemed like miles before the numbers flashed 10,000. Ten thousand miles in the past year.

Our first car was a hand-me-down from Nana, a gold '78 Thunderbird that we christened the Queen Mary. Our next car, a white Ford Escort, was called the Whitestar (prone to accidents) and the following blue Escort we called the Batmobile. But when Papa and I got the Vue last year, we just kept waiting for a name to inspire us, and after ten thousand miles, we were still waiting. Ten thousand miles earlier, we had been driving a budget compact, we had the duplets living with us, and we had just made arrangements for Kyle to come home. Ten thousand miles earlier, our biggest worry had been whether Kyle would get out of the hospital. Ten thousand miles earlier, we spent every night at the Neonatal Intensive Care Unit, singing show tunes to a baby boy missing his intestines and wondering whether he would ever eat like a normal baby.

Ten thousand miles earlier, all we knew was that we were caring for three babies, one of whom might not live, and all we could do was put one mile on top of the other, doing what we could for the triplets.

A week before the odometer milestone, one of the deputies I work with saw me getting into the car. He said,

"I always took you for a soccer mom."

It *was* a soccer mom kind of car. The car was just one of the ways that Papa and I changed. A lot of people said that I was gentler than I used to be. I didn't cut off quite as many cars, and I didn't accelerate through yellow lights anymore. I had the kids in the back of the car and kids gave me a conscience. I even found myself letting cars in at a merge.

I liked being gentle. I liked smiling and waving the pedestrian on, even when I thought that he was taking his sweet time walking across the street. In ten thousand miles, I had become just a little more patient.

That patience sometimes even accompanied me into the house. Some nights I didn't get any housework done at all, and the closest thing to cooking I could manage was dialing Geneva Pizza. But I had the patience to sit in the living room and read *The Cat in the Hat* because even though Joshua and Vivienne didn't understand the words, they liked the sound of my voice. (Kyle just liked the way the book tasted.)

Ten thousand miles earlier, I'd begun to allow for the small possibility that there was a point to being on this planet, and that my purpose just might be raising the triplets. Ten thousand miles earlier my carefully grown cynicism began to fall apart and I found myself thinking that maybe, just maybe, there was a force that I didn't understand that made the wheels go round.

THE HEARING would start the next day at one-thirty at Department 14 in Juvenile Court on Fallon Street in Oakland. The hearing would be in several parts. The first part would be about the mother's suitability to parent; Papa and I, as well as the social workers and the doctors, would be testifying. A lot of very mean lawyers were going to deny that she was a diagnosed schizophrenic who had been seen abusing her children. The second part, which would not start before Tuesday, would only take place if the judge decided that the mother was not capable.

We were all of us — me, Papa, Vivienne, Kyle, Joshua, Wolfcub, Miss Grrrl, maybe even Uncle Jon and Uncle Tim — in that big blue sports utility vehicle and we all weren't sure where we were going. I liked to think that the future was bright. I liked to think we had all learned a little about positive thinking and about faith. I liked to think this story could have a happy ending. I liked to think we had a million miles more to go together.

CHAPTER 15

Statue Left Behind

March 30, 2004

IT WAS like Perry Mason, without the jury. Or the justice. Judge Gee had been mysteriously replaced by a woman with impossibly copper hair who brusquely announced, "My docket is very busy, so we won't spend much time on this case. A day at most. Let me start by limiting testimony."

On the right hand side of the court, Ned Summerfield, the lawyer we had been spending our life savings on, wearing a gray suit, and pale blue tie, clutched his brown leather briefcase. I wore my one and only suit: blue wool, starched white cotton shirt, striped necktie. Papa, who did not own a suit, wore one of my shirts, with a purple silk tie.

On the left hand side: three lawyers, one for the county (Ms. Wong), one for the triplets, one for the birth mother. Sitting with them was Cici, in a sleeveless shirt and jeans.

Her medication was off that day, and she kept shaking her head from side to side. The birth grandmother sat behind her, prepared to cry on the right cue.

Behind us: a panoply of social workers, each of them rooting that expediency beat out justice.

Absent: the triplets, disallowed from the room where the rest of their lives would be settled.

The judge started: "First we will call a social worker to testify about the mother's mental health."

"Your honor," Ned started, "Should we not be asking a psychiatrist questions about mental health?"

"This court does not have the time for psychiatrists. Proceed."

Ms. Wong called up a social worker, a woman in a gray silk suit. She had never seen the triplets. Two weeks earlier, she had testified that the birth mother was mentally ill, and should never be left alone with the children.

"In your expert opinion, is this woman fit to parent?"

The social worker turned toward the judge, "This is a miracle of modern times. This woman is cured of all mental illness."

Ned stood, "Excuse me, your honor, but I object. Leading mental health research states that Schizophrenia can be stabilized, but it cannot be cured."

The judge frowned. Ms. Wong looked at the gray-haired lawyer for the triplets. "We do not believe that she ever was a schizophrenic."

Cici giggled.

"But the medical history —"

Ms. Wong pounced, "— is sealed and is not a matter of court record."

Ned persisted. "But your honor, we have seen evidence that Ms. Cruz abandoned the children in the hospital."

Ms. Wong looked at the heavyset lawyer for the birth mother, who offered, "She was confused at the time."

"Confused does not excuse walking out on your newborn premature children," Ned challenged, "one of whom was having heart surgery and his intestines removed."

The judge frowned again. She pulled up her black sleeve, looked at her watch, and asked the witness, "Have you observed this woman?"

"Well, all the notes indicate that she is participating in her treatment plan. I have the notes from Samuel King, who reports that she has made great progress with the children."

"But have *you* ever seen her with the children?"

"That's not relevant," Ms. Wong insisted. The judge nodded.

"Have you ever seen her shaking the babies?" Ned asked.

The social worker said quietly, "That may be explained

by normal cultural behavior."

"You may step down," Ms. Wong said.

The judge looked again at her watch. "Mr. Summerfield, do you have any evidence to present?"

"I have an attachment expert, who can testify that even at this early age each of the triplets have demonstrated signs of fear of the birth mother —" Ned began.

"I don't have time for that. I have another case on the docket this afternoon." She shook her head.

"Three doctors have volunteered to testify that the children's health and recovery had been, in large measure, a function of these two men and a year without sleep."

"Irrelevant," the judge announced

"Well then, your honor, at least let one of these men testify."

The judge sighed, "Proceed."

I sweated through the suit as I walked up to the stand. The court report said, "Please state your name for the record."

"My name is Kevin Thaddeus Paulson."

"Mr. Paulson," Ned started, "Have you ever seen this woman with the Cruz triplets?"

"Yes, I have."

"What was she like?"

"Well, she shook the children. She shouted at them. She drove them around in a car without any car seats. She deliberately ignored the doctor's orders."

"And why did Samuel King, the social worker, not report this?"

"Most of the time he was out of the room. He said that he had a busy schedule."

Ms. Wong stood up, "Objection. Irrelevant."

"Sustained."

"Mr. Paulson, why are you fighting so hard to keep these children?"

"Because… because I love them. And I do not believe that they would be safe with the birth mother."

Mr. Summerfield stepped down to allow the cross examination. Ms. Wong stood up, pointed her finger in my face. "Mr. Paulson, isn't it true that you call these children by names other than the birth names?"

"Yes."

"Why would you do that?"

"Because the first eleven social workers told us to do that."

"Isn't it true that you obstructed reunification? That you purposely hindered the visits?"

Ned stood up, "Your honor, I have here a record that the Paulsons kept of the visits. Cici did not show up eight times, and showed up late fourteen times. Mr. King was not there for more than half of the visits."

The judge looked at her watch, and said, grimly, "I

will rule on this matter at two-thirty."

NED LEFT us in peace, more or less, for lunch. Papa and
I sat in a Starbucks in Oakland, neither one of us saying a
word, neither one of us sipping our lattés.

The hour and a half passed somehow.

We walked back into the courtroom. The three lawyers
in opposition were laughing, and Ms. Wong smiled broadly
as we walked in. Cici was reading *Seventeen* magazine. The
birth grandmother was talking on a cell phone. The bailiff
called the court into session.

The judge sat down and said, "I have carefully reviewed the testimony, and the notes from Mr. King. From
what the social worker has testified, Ms. Cruz has made
tremendous progress, and has proven her dedication to
her children. The Cruz triplets will move back in with her
effective at five p.m. today. Ms. Cruz, it is obvious to me
that these two men (indicating Papa and me) have spent an
enormous amount of time and energy on these children,
and that the children are strongly bonded to them. I cannot
order you to do so, but I strongly encourage that you
remain in contact with them, for the sake of the children."

Not one person in the court believed that she ever
would.

Ms. Wong clicked shut her briefcase. Papa and I each
shook Ned's hand. Papa had manners, and so he turned to

Cici, trying to keep his voice together, trying not to cry, and said, "Good luck. If there is anything we can do, let me know."

Cici giggled.

Ms. Wong clicked shut her briefcase, smiling broadly. Papa had manners; I did not. I stared at her, and for just one second, she saw me as I was. I said, "I hope that you can sleep at night." Papa tugged my wrist, getting me out of there while I could still hold it together.

We walked to the parking lot, and as I got into the Vue, I called Uncle Jon. Blood thrummed against my eardrums. My heart pounded in a strange staccato rhythm. My voice warbled, like it wasn't even part of me anymore. "Jon. We lost. The kids leave in two hours. Call everybody. Tell them to say goodbye."

One last manic trip across the bridge, willing each car out of my way, to the last hour I would ever see my children. Gray mist settled around the blue bungalow. We walked in the door. Uncle Jon and Aunt Dorla and Aunt Lori and Uncle Tim sat in the living room, rolling a ball back and forth to Kyle. Uncle Jon put Joshua down and looked at the other three adults, who stood up in silence and walked to the door. Uncle Tim whispered in my ear, "Call me."

I picked up Vivienne, who was crying, and all at once, Papa and I were alone and the kids were hungry. I heated up three bottles, we fed them Cheerios at the kitchen table, changed them, and then we all sat down on the couch. We spent a few more minutes as a family, with each baby crawling over us on the big old leather couch and the dogs wagging their tails in the blue bungalow on Winding Way.

The doorbell rang. At the door was the social worker who had just perjured herself. She had a sport sedan parked across the street, engine still running.

Papa said, "This is it." He picked up Vivienne and walked to the van. I picked up Joshua and Kyle and followed. Joshua burbled. Kyle gripped my index finger with all his strength. The social worker said, "It has car seats but I really don't know how they work." Brian strapped Vivienne in and she smiled, thinking this was just another trip to church or the grocery store. Joshua clapped his hands together, his newest trick. I strapped Kyle into the car seat. He knew. He looked at me with his thousand-year-old eyes and told me he knew there would never again be another session of reading *The Cat in the Hat* to the dogs. There would never again be another session of drinking formula in the rocking chair near the fireplace. Never again would the two of us sit in the dark at three in the morning, singing *Gilligan's* theme. He started crying. And I started crying.

As we walked back to the house to get their suitcases, the social worker said, "There's no room in the car for that (pointing out the doll that Nurse Vivian had crocheted) or that (the suitcase with the green velour dragon pajamas)."

Clutched in my hand was the chipped plaster statue of Saint Jude. "Can they bring just this? To watch over them?"

"They won't need it. Now they will have a real mother to watch over them."

Kyle still stared at me. I think the old soul in him was telling me that he would survive, that he had lived through heart surgery and infections and an ileostomy, and that he would take care of his brother and sister for me. I whispered to him, "It's okay to go on to this new life. May you have every joy possible. It's okay to forget us, but whether you remember or not, you will always be Kyle Thaddeus Fisher-Paulson, the boy who lived despite all odds."

The social worker slammed the door. The engine roared. Somewhere in the west the sun dropped out of the sky.

CHAPTER 16

Spring Forward, Fall Behind

She took my triplets in a sports sedan,
back to the woman who had broken them.
She would not take the chipped plaster Saint Jude.

My baby girl watched the violet sapling,
a California lilac, not old enough for shade.
She took my triplets in a sports sedan.

My middle boy could not, would not see
that fog was falling as the blue house faded,
She would not take the chipped plaster Saint Jude.

My boy with the oldest eyes watched me,
his colostomy scar a broken red.
She took my triplets in a sports sedan.

This ancient child could speak one word: Daddy.
He whispered once as she turned on the road,
She would not take the chipped plaster Saint Jude.

Dogs still barked. Horns still honked on Winding Way,
She would not take the chipped plaster Saint Jude.
I opened a box of wine, could not pray.
She took my triplets in a sports sedan.

THE FIRST night without the kids, it did not rain. Darkness closed around the blue bungalow. Miss Grrrl sat on my lap. The telephone rang. We did not answer it.

Brian said, "I'll be back in a few minutes," and a half hour later, walked in the door with a carton of Marlboros. While he was out, I sent an e-mail to all the community stating simply, "The triplets are gone. Can't really talk about it now."

The phone rang again. We looked at each other and then at the phone, let the message machine take all the condolences. The night passed without either of us sleeping.

The next morning, I packed up the strollers, the blankets, and the diapers. I dropped things off at the charity store. I left the doll on Maureen's doorstep. She'd had a baby girl, and I thought that it would make Nurse Vivian happy that some little girl had the doll.

On Friday morning, I went back to work at County Jail #7. On Saturday morning, I took a test for a promotion, having not studied for it. Other sergeants looked at me, and almost no one talked. At last, Lieutenant Ridgeway, the only other gay man of rank in the department, walked up to me and said, "I'm so sorry. We all had such hopes." And I realized that the part of me that held hope was broken.

But life goes on, even when you cannot believe.

April 3, 2004

This would be the night that brought Daylight Savings time. The next day, all I needed to do was get up, throw on a pair of jeans, and sing a couple of Hosannas. I didn't even have to believe in them. That next day would also be Palm Sunday, the beginning of Holy Week, and the end of six and a half weeks of Lent. Those forty days were meant to signify the forty days alone in the desert, and Palm Sunday (or Passion Sunday) began the week when life was renewed, when we returned from that desert.

Every culture has a celebration of the end of the darkness and the rebirth of hope. The Greeks have the spring myth of the beautiful mortal Persephone. Hades, the God of the Dead, took such a liking to the mortal that he invited her to hang out at his place, a burg that we know of as Hell. Demeter, Persephone's mother, was furious.

Being the goddess of the Harvest, and in a power position herself, she informed Hades that he wouldn't be keeping her daughter captive. And Hades said, "Finders keepers."

Demeter replied, "Fine. If I'm not happy, nobody's happy." She put a stop to all harvests: no wheat, no corn, no grapes. Which meant no wine, and before you knew it, everybody was talking about it, even Dionysius. He told the big boss Zeus. So Zeus said, "Demeter, go to hell. Literally. Go down there and get your daughter. Just make sure that she hasn't eaten anything down there. If she has broken bread with the dead, she must stay with the dead."

Demeter rushed down to Hell, and found her daughter, Persephone. But while Persephone was sitting around waiting to be rescued, she got a little on the peckish side and took a bite of a pomegranate. She ate only a third of it but that was enough. Hades told Demeter that he could have her daughter back on Earth, but that because she had eaten that third of a fruit, she must spend a third of the year with him in hell. And for that third of the year, Demeter mourned and gave no harvest. But at the time when her daughter came back from Hell (which just happened to coincide with the first full moon after the vernal equinox), Demeter celebrated with the first fruits and the first flowers.

AND SO, the day before the clock sprung forward, Brian mowed the lawn in our tiny backyard. The lilacs were in bloom, heavy and purple-scented, and the calla lilies bloomed in brilliant white crescents. The flagstones we'd made last Christmas lay in the middle of the yard. The Ceanothus trees we planted at Father's Day, one each for Kyle, Joshua and Vivienne were, ironically enough, blooming this weekend.

Kyle, Joshua, and Vivienne no longer existed. They had become Seamus, Angel, and Poppy, and they lived a life we could not share. But we had eaten the pomegranate together, and the piece of their souls that will always be Kyle and Joshua and Vivienne will be remembered in the leaves with the purple buds of the Ceanothus.

We suffered through the season in hell but we had eaten a third of the pomegranate. We went on. We needed that season to remind ourselves that there is a spring.

Finally I woke up one day and I realized that I was no longer angry, that the anger I gave up for Lent had dissipated. Maybe, just maybe, we had scared Cici enough so that she would keep herself clean and sober. Maybe she would take her medication. Maybe, just maybe, she would be willing to make sacrifices herself.

Doctor Butler had said, "Kyle would not be alive without the help and the love that you gave him." So in the middle of the night, I consoled myself with the hope that Kyle is destined for greatness. God went through extraordinary measures to keep that boy alive, even getting an old queen like me to spend the night in an emergency room singing the sound track to *Gypsy*. Surely the universe must have big plans for Kyle.

Brian and I went on a date for the first time in a very long time. Of course we had dinner at Yet Wah's. But for the first time ever, the General Kung Pao Chicken held no interest for me. Eerily, the fortune cookie was blank, no fortune inside.

We watched a stupid, romantic movie, the kind that Brian likes. I was okay until the little girl in the row in front of me turned around and started saying "DaDa. DaDa." I started crying again but quickly stopped when I realized that someone might think that I was responding emotionally to the movie.

Brian got better every day. I got better every day. We had crawled through the desert and started looking around for hope.

CHAPTER 17

In the Family Way

June 2, 2004

THERE IS no answer; there are only better questions. If you think that you've gotten to the right answer, then you've come to the wrong conclusion somewhere along the way. The trick in life is that you'll never figure out where you are going. You might as well enjoy the journey.

Two months passed. Even if we never saw them again, we could console ourselves with the fact that we saved the lives of three children. If we never knew more about them than that, then that was just part of the big mystery. We might find clues from time to time, but there were some mysteries not meant to be solved.

We spent a week or two dismantling our lives as parents, foisting the cribs and such off on our expectant friends. And in the meantime, our friends stood around doing what they do best: caring for us and giving us the space to heal. Jon invited us out for glasses of wine. Amanda flew us across the country, out to her home in the Catskills for a weekend of pinochle and reminiscence. Amanda was my oldest friend in the world, and sitting at her kitchen table, drinking coffee and putting together a jigsaw puzzle, a little of the emptiness became quiet. Most of the weekend I was fine, until Amanda suggested we go apple picking. We drove to an old orchard, and Amanda popped in the CD player her recording of the revival of *Gypsy,* and all I could think of was the waiting room at Children's Hospital.

We flew back to San Francisco. The parish allowed me to stand in the loft of our church, sobbing every time the choir sang the Hosanna that Kyle liked.

A couple of other crises helped distract us. Miss Grrrrl's one remaining kidney was struggling and she required more than her daily subcutaneous injections. The doctors suspected that Wolfcub might have a tumor and were doing blood work on him because his calcium level was elevated.

The biggest crisis was Tim: he'd been in and out of the hospital three or four times, with pneumocystis pneumonia and macrobacterial avian complex. Hard to see him like this, wasting away. Seventeen years before, he was the most vibrant person I knew, organizing ACTUP protests, assembling a Wiccan coven, writing novels, and picking up loose men. And here he was at less than a hundred and fifty pounds, slowly going blind. One night in the hospital, Tim said, "That spell on the triplets, that whatever happened they would be safe and happy? I think that was the last of my magic."

"You, Gandalf? Never!"

"This does not mean I am out of tricks...."

I wrote about hope. And it took me a while to figure out what it was that I was still hopeful about. Harvey Milk, the first gay politician to be elected to public office, lost seven elections before he won his seat on the Board of Supervisors. In the last lost election, his opponent, Art Agnos, said after the results were in, "Harvey, you know a lot about the issues, and you can tell everybody what's wrong. But you make a mistake. You gotta give 'em hope." And that is what Harvey did. He decided to walk in hope, not to focus on loss but to tell people about what could be.

Brian went on another dance tour, this time to Colorado, and while he was gone, I hired an artisan to remove the two milk glass windows and replace them with stained glass windows, each of them an opalescent white rose against a Batman blue border, each of the roses bearing three thorns. In this way, even the bungalow could remember.

We returned from our season in hell, still looking for

pomegranates. A part of me would always be broken, but the practical part of me, the Demeter, will always go back to the real world.

After we returned from New York, I told Brian that I wanted to do this again. Pigs make the best bacon, after all, and it seemed that Brian and I made fairly adequate parents. Brian said, "I need a minute to think about that." He took six weeks. The calculus of grief is different for each of us.

I went down to San Diego for a Police Leadership seminar. Part of that staying-in-motion therapy that I was working out involved going to seminars that I didn't care much about, but might do some good. First time Brian was alone in the bungalow since we lost, and I was a little worried, so I called every night. On the third night, he called me. "I went to Yet Wah's."

"Without me?"

"Without you. Without Tim. Without the triplets. It felt weird ordering the Kung Pao Chicken knowing you weren't going to finish it. Know what my fortune said? "

"Help! I'm a prisoner in a Chinese bakery?"

"Prepare yourself for a change of events in your personal life."

"Really? You do know it's a sacrilege to make up fortune cookie fortunes."

A long breath at the other end of the phone. "I'm not

ready. I'm never gonna be ready. But you're right. Let's start exploring again." We toasted, clinking glasses against the phone receivers.

We thought about going to another agency. I called a few and was surprised to find that even during these supposedly modern times, many agencies were perfectly content to place children with adoptive parents, so long as the parents had opposing genders. But we eventually decided that we liked the people at A Better Way. So the morning I got back from Southern California, we went back to visit Meredith, and we talked about another placement.

Meredith said, "Unlike the first placement, this one will take months to complete." We'd learned a lot since then. Children were brought under the care of Child Protective Services when a social worker decided that the birth parent was unable to care for the child, whether it is because of neglect, death, drug abuse or psychiatric issues. At first, the county offered reunification services to the birth parents, and the children were placed in foster homes while they gave the parents the time to get off of drugs, get out of jail, or deal with whatever condition that resulted in the loss of their kids. There were multiple hearings to determine the birth parent's progress. After a year of this, the court would hold a permanency hearing, called a 26 hearing. At this hearing the court decided whether the children should be returned to the birth parents or if an alternative placement plan should be made. In most cases, the alternative placement plan was adoption.

Brian told Meredith, "We're ready to explore another placement but we have a few conditions."

I clarified: "The child must be discovered in a rocket ship with documentation that all other inhabitants of the planet Krypton have perished."

Always more reasonable than I, Brian simply requested that the child be as close as possible to the 26 hearing.

We were again asked about age, gender, and race. We replied that we had just fostered health-compromised triplets from two different genders and two different races, so we thought we could handle any combination. Meredith then handed us "The Book," a list of all the kids in the surrounding counties available for placement.

It felt a little like catalog shopping. There we were, flipping through page after page of children in need of love, and all Meredith asked was, "Place a post-it next to each kid you think might be a good match."

A large percentage of children in the system were of African American descent; in California many were of Hispanic descent. Because a lot of adoptive parents want single, blond, blue-eyed, healthy babies, the system had more difficulty placing kids of mixed race, kids who were older, health-compromised, or in sibling sets. While

Brian looked mainly at the sibling placements, I fell in love with all of the kids and within twenty minutes had gone through a pad of post-its.

Three hours later, we had looked at every child in need of a home in ten neighboring counties. Meredith took down the list of children we were interested in and sent out notes of inquiry to the social workers on those cases. The next step would be meeting some of these kids, at which point, they'd get to decide on us, and we'd get to decide on them. When would we get an answer? No one knew. It was still part of the mystery. But the important thing was this: We were siding with hope. We were trying again.

The second step was even stranger. Every six months or so, the neighboring counties in the Bay Area throw a "matching" picnic, where they invite potential adoptive parents and potential adoptees and watch as we interact. Brian, as it turned out, was dancing in Hawaii that week (yes, the poor thing!), and so I went to this peculiar rite alone. Well, actually not alone; I went with another gay couple who were also looking to adopt. I spent the bulk of the day feeling like I was back in South Ozone Park.

Unlike my older brothers, Earl and Donald, who were fairly athletic growing up, I was a nelly-queen-in-training. My brothers were ten and eight years older than me and ran the Irish hooligans who lived on the 130th block of Sutter Avenue, meaning that the two of them organized every stoopball, basketball, and stickball game on the block. Using a broom handle in place of a bat, the game always began with one brother throwing the stick to the other brother. They then went hand over hand until one of them reached the top of the stick with his thumb. This brother got to pick whom he wanted on his team first. Donald always picked Tommy McCormick and Earl always picked Jimmy Cadden. After that, they chose from all the other McCormick Brothers, the McCafferys, the Caddens, Michael Carbone and Martin Campisi. Then it was just Patrick Cadden and me. Donald fretted if he got the last pick, but Earl always went straight to Patrick Cadden, who was four years younger than me, and, if you ask me, just as nelly, but that would be the artisanal pot calling the kettle lavender.

Hence, I spent a lot of my youth acting as first base umpire.

It felt a bit like I was acting as first base umpire again at the matching picnic, with all the pretty parents talking to all the pretty children. Meredith told me to just stick it out so I actually talked to a lot of kids and fell in love with each of them.

Nothing substantial materialized from any of those matches, but then serendipity kicked in. During the fight for the triplets, we met a lot of social workers, some evil and some nice. Unfortunately, none of the nice social workers had legal standing in the case.

Ellen, who worked for Alameda County, was one of the nice ones. She decided that she wanted us to have more children. She saw us take three medically fragile children into our home and she saw them flower. She considered what happened during the trial a crime. The moment she heard we were back "on the market," she called A Better Way. She had found a baby boy who would make a perfect Fisher-Paulson.

Here is what we knew: He was nine months old, his mother had a history of crack and methamphetamine abuse, and his father was in prison. There was no history of mental illness. His 26 hearing was scheduled for June 16, meaning that he would be legally freed for adoption six months after that. Ellen really wanted us to have this baby boy.

He was, by the way, African American. One of the other gay couples whom we met at the agency had told us that it would be very hard for an African American boy to grow up with two white men, because he would face the prejudices of both the black and white communities as well as the straight and gay communities. I hesitated for a moment. Funny that the Mexican/Pakistani triplets had never caused comment with anyone.

Ozone Park, which was not too far from where

Archie Bunker lived, had strong racial divisions. I grew up thinking that African Americans were very different. There was only one black child in my school, a girl named Elizabeth, who sat next to me in the third grade. No one else in the class wanted to sit next to her. Of course no one wanted to sit next to me either. I was a marked man, or should I say marked queen. No one wanted to sit next to the boy with the Barbie lunchbox.

Elizabeth was my partner in being outcasts. We had a nativity pageant at Christmas time, and Sister Mary Magdalene cast every single one of us except Elizabeth and me. Elizabeth's Kris Kringle never materialized with her gift at the grab bag. One of the Stallone sisters had my name and I got a plastic crucifix and a coloring book about the night before Christmas. I gave Elizabeth that crucifix and together we drew in the coloring book while the other kids rehearsed the Nativity. One of the tough kids in the class asked me, "Why'd you do that? Don't you know she's a n-…" It was the first time I had ever heard that word.

But not the last. Fifteen years later, while my college choir was on tour in New Orleans, a tour guide mentioned how "lazy" the blacks were when discussing labor in the south. Upon seeing the look of shock on our faces — including the other Kevin in the choir, an African American tenor — she quickly amended her statement: "But not black like you are. This kind was real black, shiny black."

This became a standard joke with the choir. When we sang a spiritual, we asked the conductor whether this was traditional Black Gospel or Shiny Black Gospel. Kevin used to kid me that I was not like other white people; I was shiny white.

So here I was, without any answers. But a new mystery awaited. We asked Meredith if we could meet the boy.

CHAPTER 18

Avec Beau

"What's in a name? That which we call a rose by
any other name would smell as sweet."
— ROMEO AND JULIET

June 12, 2004

WHAT IS in a name? Fifteen years ago, we named Miss Grrrrl on the day we met her. Diva was named during a subway ride with Amanda. On three hours' notice we came up with first and middle names for the triplets. Brian and I worked best under pressure; in the absence of pressure we procrastinated. We also both put great store in naming. For me, it is the *raison d'etre* of the poet: to name things. It is second only to creation in the magic of this world.

My own names have defined me. When I was a kid, Nurse Vivian called me Kevin Thaddeus, emphasizing the

Thaddeus part as a tribute to Saint Jude Thaddeus. My father called me Noodle Nose. I'm not sure why he went with this name because although my nose is large and decidedly crooked, it bears no resemblance to a noodle. My brothers called me Sputnik, as I was exactly the same age as that artificial satellite. The neighborhood kids called me Porky, in tribute to my childhood addiction to potato chips with mayonnaise. Cruelly accurate, it shapes my self-image to this day. I worked hard to escape "Porky" and for years took any other nickname I could get, so long as it was kosher.

By the time I got to Notre Dame, I had lost a lot of weight. I was tired of others making up nicknames for me, so I chose my own. Nowadays, people think I got it from Knute Rockne or Dan Devine or Joe Montana but truth to tell, I picked the name "Kip" because it had the right balance of prep and perk, two attributes needed for the construction of my new personality.

Baptisms are relative. A community chooses to call a person by a certain name because the parents said so (Kevin), or because the community said so (Porky) or because the individual said so (Kip). In a very real sense, I was born again with each re-naming. I continued to be the same old me, but with each baptism, I got a little bit wiser, a little bit more in touch with my soul, and little bit closer to whatever force works the universe. One of the deputies at work recently informed me that everyone called me "Super P" as a way to let me know that I was part of their community, that we shared certain values, that they respected me for the ways in which I was different from other little deputies, but that I was like them, that I also believed in something as old fashioned as justice. There was another sergeant where I worked who did not have a nickname. They called her "Ma'am," making it clear that the community of peace officers recognized that she held herself as different from them. I was Super P because they knew I liked comic books, they knew I respected them, and they knew that I acted responsibly in relation to the community.

We were Daddy and Papa when the triplets lived with us. We reverted back to Brian and Kevin when they were given back to their birth mother. We were ready to be re-baptized as Daddy and Papa.

On Wednesday we drove over to A Better Way and met the newest addition to the Fisher-Paulson family. He was adorable and sweet, with two perfectly formed dimples. He crawled non-stop for an hour and a quarter, then landed on Brian's lap and fell asleep. Hooked, Brian asked when he could move to the blue bungalow. Of course, we'd have to get through a legal hurdle first: his 26 hearing was scheduled for the next Wednesday. He would be cleared for legal adoption if the hearing was successful and six months later, the persons that he'd live with would *legally* be called his parents.

We went through all four thousand names in our baby name book and culled them down to a hundred names, then fifty names, then fourteen names, then ten names. One of the few things Papa and I have in common is that we can both be stubborn. His excuse was a Maine heritage; I had mule Irish genes. Thus, when we got down to two potential names for the new baby, we settled in on opposing sides of the equation. We felt the awesome weight of calling this guy a new name for the rest of the 21st century and we wanted to make sure that he got the right one.

The court recognized the power of a name as well, which is why, after the 26 hearing, they conducted a brief naming ceremony, where the judge would ask the prospective parents by what name they would call the child. Two days after the 26 hearing, the kid could move in. We were both committed to having a name by that time. And he would grow up knowing that our particular village was taking responsibility for raising him. A week or so after the adoption, we planned to hold a christening (or wiccaning, if Uncle Time got his way), in which we recognized that he was a new member of our community, and we'd officially choose to call him by the name that Papa and I finally chose. And we, in turn, would re-baptize everyone in our community as Aunts and Uncles once again.

I had suggested Harold, after my father, and Papa countered with Jerry, his father, or Wesley, his grandfather. I doubled back with Aloysius, my father's middle name, and he started in on the Jarods and Jeromes. We exhausted the family names: my father's name is Harold Aloysius, my grandfather's name is George, my brother's name is Earl, and Brian's grandfather's name was Ronald Wesley Fairbanks. None of those names sounded like they were going to last very long in the schoolyard.

Brother Earl suggested Sansbeaux, as a variation of Sambo, remembering Nurse Vivian reading golden books in South Ozone Park. "Kevin," he said, "nowadays we joke about Little Black Sambo, but I remember he was the guy who outsmarted the tigers."

My one semester of French, however, made the decision for me. This allowed me to translate Sansbeaux as *without beauty,* a name that certainly does not apply to my kid. No, this child was a great beauty, but Avec Grande Beau, or *With Great Beauty*, seemed a little awkward. But this child would always be my beauty. And my hope.

I thanked Earl and suggested that he save the name for the next time that he adopted a horse. But I was very grateful that Earl had taken the time to think. In fact, since I announced that Brian and I were taking this boy in, there had been a conspicuous silence from most of the Paulson family. In many ways, I understood that silence. At forty-something, we were a little long in the tooth to be adopting a baby. But Brian and I never did things the easy way.

Our neighbors and our co-workers were remembering the history of the past six months. The comment that hurt the most was from one of the sergeants at work, "Are you really going to adopt him this time?"

Second worst comment came from the neighbor two doors down: "Don't you think you guys are doing this a little quickly? You haven't really mourned your loss."

In truth, you *never* really finish mourning that kind of loss. There would always be a vast and dark grief inside me. I would never forget them. If any of the three called me twenty years from now, I would give them whatever they asked, because they will always be family.

The simple truth was that sometimes life did not work out as I planned. I had two choices: either get stuck in my pain or move forward and hope to make another kind of joy. That is what we chose. We chose hope. We chose to believe that if you keep doing the right thing, everything will work out positively. As for whether or not things were gonna work out this time, we couldn't know.

Which brought us to the little bit of frustrating news. On Wednesday, Brian and I finished the overnight visit, brought our new son back to his regular placement, and awaited the results of the 26 hearing. When I got to A Better Way, our social worker was frowning. As it turns out, the 26 hearing could not be held without the birth parents being present. In this case, the birth father, who was currently in custody, was supposed to be transferred from his current jail for the hearing. Somebody screwed up and he wasn't transferred, meaning the judge had to reschedule the hearing. Our social worker told us not to worry, that it was just a legal glitch and everything was proceeding on course. But of course we worried. I had hoped that our son would soon be legally free for adoption, but the truth of the matter was that the court controlled the date and the universe was working overtime to teach us lessons in patience.

I dropped our son off with the social worker, who brought him to his temporary foster home for two more days. When the social worker arrived, the foster mother was not there, but there was a very strange man standing at the door who said he could take the baby. So the social worker, quite rightly, said "Thanks, but no thanks," and got back in the car. The county social worker called our social worker who said, "Well, we'll just move them in with Brian and Kevin today."

Brian responded to crises much better than I. I've seen him change an ileostomy bag on two hours sleep, drive from New York to Maine in a blizzard, and dance a *pas de deux* on a broken ankle. Papa calmly said, "We can do this. Pick up the baby. We'll get the groceries tomorrow. Oh, and by the way, his name is Zane. Zane Thaddeus." And thus a family was born. Somewhere in a china cabinet, a Saint Jude statue was smiling that yet another Paulson child had the same middle name. And the patron of the impossible had another impossible Paulson to look out for.

Eight or nine years from now, when he gets around to asking me how he got his name, I will undoubtedly concoct a charming story about Zane Grey being a distant cousin or my great love for *Citizen Kane* or how it is an acronym for Zsa Zsa Gabor, Arlene Francis, Nanette Fabre and Eve Arden, our favorite actresses. I might even say that it's the masculine form of Jane. I might say that we picked Zane Thaddeus because it can be abbreviated to Z'eus. I might ask, a la Bette Davis, "Whatever Happened to Baby Zane?"

The truth of the matter is that we liked the feel of the name: Zane. Solid. One syllable. Unique.

And we, of course, were Daddy and Papa again.

Ghosts of Christmas Past

December 17, 2007

THREE AND a half years passed. Papa and I adopted Zane and fostered another boy who we named Aidan (so we could go from Z to A) and he was also adopted. We took in rescue dogs and we did get legally married, and that legality lasted for a few months. And then got challenged. And then got validated again, by the Supreme Court. All that is the stuff of another book.

Tim passed away a few months after we adopted Zane. He made an annoying ghost, waiting until I was feeling agnostic to pounce.

Before his Wiccan phase, Tim had been fascinated by Castaneda. He flew to Hawaii for a Castaneda conference, slept on the beach for four days and came home telling me to watch out for my dreams. If, for instance, you were having a dream about a tea party and you saw a fish, you'd need to watch the fish because it's most likely the key to the mystic realm. The moment you realize that you are looking at the fish is the moment you realize that you are dreaming and then you enter the waking dream state. Got it?

Tim haunted my dreams; he was the fish out of place. Each time I saw him, I looked right at him and said, "Wait a minute. You're dead. You're the thing that doesn't belong in the dream."

And in every dream, Tim rolled his eyes, lit a cigarette and said, "Well, it took you long enough to figure that one out."

When I told Aunt Lori about these dreams, I expected her to write them off since she was almost as cynical as I was about metaphysics. Instead she allowed that she was also having dreams about Tim. In all of them, he asked her to play cribbage, each time insisting that he would "peg the heck" out of her.

Tim and I played cribbage together for about twenty years. He was ruthless. He allowed me to get about fifteen points ahead before he just "pegged the heck" out of me. He usually beat me by thirty points (known to all cribbage players as a skunk). I asked Lori what she thought of the dream, and she told me that he must want us to play cribbage together. None of us had played for the cribbage queen ornament since the last night that Tim and I played cribbage in the hospital. He double skunked me. I said, "You better not gloat or I won't get the nurse when it's time for morphine."

Tim replied, "Why gloat? It's not like I can take the cribbage ornament where I'm going."

On Friday night, I started talking back to Tim in my dreams. I said, "You know, if you're going to all the trouble of haunting me, you could at least be clear about what you're haunting about. We got a lot going on here." The next morning, we received a package from Maine. Tim's sister had sent us Nells, the incredibly delicate paper-thin cookies he had requested on his death bed.

WE HOSTED the Ornament Party on a Saturday night. The first guest arrived at about five o'clock and the last left at about one in the morning. In those eight hours we sipped mulled wine and ate lumpia and pancit and these supposedly low-calorie snacks made by Aunt Dee with pecans, chocolate, and pretzels in them. I hope they were low-cal, because I finished the plate.

Zane and Aidan were angels. Well, relative angels. Nothing got broken. Uncle Dave gave them Dove chocolate with almonds about fifteen minutes into the party and they zoomed until midnight.

Aidan had a genetic brother who was adopted by a Chinese/Jewish gay couple named Ming and Larry. They also came in from Alameda, and it was nice to have their children at the party, in part because Jasmine is every bit as spirited as Zane. She always gave him a run for his money. In one of the few lulls between the kids chasing the dogs and consuming chocolate, Ming told me that he was surprised to find that Aidan and Adam now had a little sister. The birth mother had entered rehab and was committed to taking care of her daughter. I brought this up with Meredith, our social worker, who was also in attendance. I asked if she had any other secrets she was keeping from us. She lost all color in her face and said, "I need to speak with you and Brian right now."

She grabbed Papa and the three of us went to the back yard. "I've known for about two months, but I haven't told you."

"Told us what?"

"The triplets were taken away from Cici. They were badly abused. They're living with an undisclosed relative. In Fresno, I think."

I had never thought that I would hear about the triplets again. I thought that story was over, that maybe I'd been wrong after all. Maybe Cici had gotten herself off the drugs, and maybe the triplets were leading a wonderful life.

Ghosts never leave you. Right before the court hearing, when we were asking for prayers, wishes, and good thoughts, Tim cast a Wiccan spell to keep the triplets connected to us. I don't know if that was a blessing or a curse. Tim was never again healthy after that spell, as if it had taken everything out of him. And me, there is a part of me that will always be broken. There is a part of me that can never quite believe again. And yet, I go on.

What had Tim been trying to tell me all those weeks? I'm not sure but I knew that tragedy was inevitable. People died; people left; couples separated. But it didn't matter how things ended as much as how things were when they were still together. It wasn't important that Tim died of AIDS; it was important that Tim pegged the heck out of me on the cribbage board. It wasn't important that Nurse Vivian died of ovarian cancer; it was important that she gave me the recipe for apple pie.

Finally, it wasn't important that the court took Joshua, Kyle, and Vivienne away from us. It was important that we gave them the love they needed. And in return, they gave us a year of joy and taught us how to be patient and kind. They gave us a year wherein we got to make a lot of mistakes that Zane and Aidan would never have to tolerate, thus making us better parents. Our capacity to love did not end that day; it changed. The triplets would always be the ghosts of our Christmas past, but now and forever, Zane and Aidan would remain our Christmas presents. ✳

FROM LEFT TO RIGHT: *Kevin, Zane, Brian, and*
Aidan Fisher-Paulson at the San Francisco
Gay Pride Day Parade, 2009

Acknowledgements

This memoir could not exist without this history, and so I would like to acknowledge my birth family (Nurse Vivian, Hap, Brother Donald and Brother Earl) as well as my chosen family (Papa, Vivienne, Joshua, Kyle, Zane, Aidan, Miss Grrrl, Diva, Wolfcub, Qp, Krypto, Buddyboy and Bandit) for making my life so interesting.

The Village that continues to raise these children is also the Village that demanded this book, including Uncle Jon, Aunt Lori and Uncle David. Somewhere in some cosmic afterlife, Uncle Tim continued to demand the book as well, and has arranged a fair number of coincidences to make it happen.

Writers such as Dorothy Allison and Cat Meads have encouraged my writing. Brianna Smith reviewed an early draft of this work, and many thanks to D. Patrick Miller for his editing, as well as to Papa for reading and re-reading and re-re-reading this until I got the dates somewhat in order. Lori read the last draft and corrected a number of my exaggerations. — *Kevin Thaddeus Fisher-Paulson*

ABOUT FEARLESS BOOKS

Fearless Books is an independent publisher in California's Napa Valley, focusing on books in the fields of contemporary spirituality, literary fiction and poetry, and quality memoirs. Although we publish few books annually, we consult, edit, and assist in the independent publishing process for many writers through Fearless Literary Services. *A Song for Lost Angels* is the first title released under our Personal History Project, in which we are seeking memoirs for editorial development with the aim of mainstream or independent publication, possibly under the Fearless imprint.

To see our current roster of print and e-books, as well as the full range of Fearless Literary Services, go to:

www.fearlessbooks.com

Made in the USA
San Bernardino, CA
16 June 2014